THE CONNAUGHT BAR

RECIPES AND ICONIC CREATIONS

AGOSTINO
PERRONE
WITH
GIORGIO BARGIANI + MAURA MILIA

THE CONNAUGHT MARTINI

100 CONNAUGHT BAR COCKTAILS

OOPS, I DROPPED THE CONNAUGHT MARTINI

Let me begin with a premise: I do not frequent cocktail bars. Rarely do I have the occasion. Therefore, I am not writing from the position of an expert when it comes to cocktail making or drinking. If I look back to my first cocktail, I've had a few breakthrough moments since then that led me to the Connaught Bar and to writing these notes.

FIRST, THE DJ YEARS

Early in my culinary career, there was a moment when I was cooking and DJing. I had opened a bar with friends. We were all into motorcycles and it was called the Harley Club. It was a place for me to unwind after work at my first restaurant. I would show up after midnight when I closed the kitchen, take off my chef's jacket and order my drink of choice. For five years I stood behind the DJ stand and started off my sets with a cold draft beer in a tall glass with a shot of vodka poured in.

The Harley Club closed in 1994. I sold my restaurant and went off to Monte Carlo to work with Alain Ducasse. One year later, I opened another restaurant, Osteria Francescana, and shortly after that married Lara Gilmore. In 2000, Beppe Palmieri joined our team to become the maître and sommelier. He did something remarkable that I had never seen. He added his own artisanal drinks to our beverage pairing. Not proper cocktails, but a combination of flavours with a dash of alcohol and lots of ice and water to match our more challenging dishes, bringing energy and freshness to the dining experience. Since then, I started seeing cocktails in a whole new light.

THEN, THERE CAME THE GIN AND TONIC YEARS

From 2005, I attended the culinary conference Lo Mejor de la Gastronomía. Those years were some of the most memorable and I am grateful for the climate of experimentation and discovery and the diffusion and sharing of ideas. Every moment presented an opportunity to build on relationships with chefs, journalists and artisans as we all witnessed the world of gastronomy changing before our eyes. Most of the socializing happened outside the conference doors in a bar called Dickens. The bartender had won awards for his version of the classic gin and tonic. That is all that I drank in those years, it is all that anyone drank – gin and tonic. Lots of them.

THE CONNAUGHT BAR

In 2010, I walked into the Connaught Bar for the first time. We were in London for the occasion of The World's 50 Best Restaurants awards. We had heard rumours about a bar run by Italian bartenders in the centre of Mayfair, so Lara and I planned to pass by before the ceremony for a 'good luck' drink. As I walked through the Connaught's lobby and the narrow hall to the Connaught Bar, I was disoriented. A hotel bar down a hallway? Shouldn't it be right there in the middle of the action? No. It felt hidden, almost like a speakeasy. What made this place so special? I was taken off guard when I entered. It did not look like a bar at all but a sleek silver-toned lounge with cozy chairs and tables and a spectacular dark green bar. No one sat at the bar. It wasn't made for sitting. It was a theatre. One where the orchestra plays the sounds of cocktails being made: ice cubes tossed in a tumbler, pouring and stirring and rhythmic shaking. And then we heard familiar voices speaking in Italian, 'Ciao!' Behind the bar, several well-dressed Italians were moving all their body parts like a perfectly choreographed dance. They were smiling, animated and busy. Nonetheless, they noticed us, 'Ciao, Massimo! Ciao, Lara!'

Agostino Perrone, Director of Mixology, introduced himself and seated us with a view of the bar. I said without thinking, 'I'll have a gin and tonic.' He looked at me and cocked his head. 'Davvero? Really?' he said. Before I knew it, a cocktail was handed to me. 'A warm-up drink,' he explained. It was red, crisp and remarkably inviting. It was certainly not a gin and tonic. And then Agostino said, 'How about a Martini?', as he pulled the Martini trolley over to our table. I do not drink Martinis, but that trolley, being one of the most beautiful objects I had ever seen, convinced me to try one. Agostino demonstrated the selection of homemade bitters and asked us to choose. I chose Dr Ago's bitters, a combination of bergamot and ginseng. Lara selected grapefruit bitters. Little did I know another chapter had just begun.

Since that day, on every trip to London and for all occasions, Lara and I pass by the Connaught Bar to say hello. When it is award season, we cannot miss our 'good luck' pre-awards cocktail. Every time it is like returning to see distant family.

When we first started going, most hotel bars were serving classic cocktails. The Connaught Bar invited a new generation of mixologists to bring those classic cocktails into the future. Agostino and his team dedicated their very first cocktail menu to the idea of the forgotten classics, paying their personal homage to the cocktail tradition. They had a wish to revive those recipes that had become obsolete and too old-fashioned by shedding light on the ingenuity behind those cocktails, which were gathering dust in books. Their menu featured surprising flavours and ingredients from the passionate study and revitalization of ancient formulas with a zest for the contemporary. They were highly aware that innovation often begins with the evolution of tradition. And so they went on, with new team members bringing their bright approach and enthusiasm over the years. (On this note, a special mention goes to Maura Milia, Bar Manager, and Giorgio Bargiani, Assistant Director of Mixology of the Connaught Bar.) Similarly, we have always conceived the kitchen at Osteria Francescana to be a laboratory and an observatory, where we look at the past in a critical way, not a nostalgic one. Our work is not about forgetting the past but finding the most appropriate way to bring it forward. The team at the Connaught Bar and Osteria Francescana share this in common.

On the subject of this synergy of thought, a few years ago, Agostino, Giorgio and I began a conversation about what a cocktail made with balsamic vinegar might taste like. I am from Modena, Italy, and balsamic vinegar is in my veins. I introduced Agostino and Giorgio to the variety of vinegars we produce and the conversation led to a brainstorm that eventually brought us to the annual Identità Golose conference in Milan in early 2022 to present Agostino and Giorgio's cocktail. When we got the chance to work together, we were perfectly aligned on the ideals we wanted to express. Experiencing a cocktail, or a dish, means savouring its past, present and future. It goes beyond taste. We jointly created, Oops, I Dropped The Balsamic. Agostino and Giorgio chose one of their most iconic drinks, the Good Fellas, with the desire to explore it from another point of view. 'Traditional balsamic vinegar,' we thought, 'What better ingredient to add to an already iconic drink?' Deeply rooted in Modenese and Italian tradition, yet timeless, versatile and vanguardist. With it, we added texture and Italianity to a masterpiece, thus bringing it to the future.

That's the only way I know to be contemporary. And it is how the Connaught Bar has managed to stay contemporary after 15 years of activity, always changing with time without ever changing its identity and perspective on the world. This book will bring you on a journey inside this iconic and revolutionary place, which – among the huge number of awards and accolades won over the years – in 2020 and 2021 ranked No. 1 on the World's 50 Best Bars list.

I have been a chef for over 30 years. My life's passion and my profession revolve around flavour, ingredients, techniques, ideas and hospitality. When I think about the Connaught Bar, I return again and again to the hospitality, the methodology and the quality experiences that I have experienced there over the past decade.

So it is to you, Agostino, Giorgio, Maura and the whole team, that I raise my glass. Not a beer with a shot of vodka. Not a gin and tonic. I choose a Connaught Martini made with Dr Ago's bitters. I toast to the past 15 years of your success and to all the wonderful years we passed with you. Thank you.

To the good luck you brought us and the good cheer. To the Martinis and the Oops! and all the cocktails to come.

In our future, there is more future. And with the Connaught Bar, it will certainly be an amazing one!

Complimenti ragazzi. Avanti sempre così!!!
Massimo Bottura

Far more than recipes, this is the creative mindset laid bare. Here, you will find the results of lifetimes devoted to a global exploration of flavour, of drinks culture, and of hospitality. But this is not simply a presentation of the world, it is the world as Ago Perrone sees it, and smells, tastes, hears and touches it. This is the world of flavour choreographed by the Connaught Bar.

For the past sixteen years, the Connaught Bar and its bar team have been celebrated around the world. What does it take to earn the title of world's best bar and to receive it again and again? It takes remarkable creativity and vision and talent and the determination to maintain the level of service, quality and the freshness of both the new concepts and the experience.

I will never forget meeting Ago at Montgomery Place off Portobello Road around 2006. In a black shirt and bright yellow braces (suspenders), he was already earning renown in the industry. But mostly he was recognized and celebrated by his peers and regular customers. Peer admiration in the drinks industry is a bellwether of success. Soon, we would find ourselves speaking from the same stages: in Amsterdam, Athens, Berlin, Moscow, New Orleans, Paris, Rome. And here, I gradually discovered the many layers of genius that make up the artistry of Ago Perrone.

I have personally tasted every drink in this book. It was one of the more pleasant tasks I have faced in my life. Added to that experience was the joy of discovering the story, the inspiration and the masterful level of execution it took to sculpt each of these creations – a team effort that involves the heart and soul and passion of each member of Ago's amazing team. If the Connaught Bar is theatre, then this book is the libretto. Meet the players, explore the melodies they create.

What brings guests back to the Connaught Bar night after night? It's in the details. Finally, here is a glimpse behind the curtain.

The Latin phrase *Placere placet*, or 'the pleasure to please', is our mantra at the Connaught. You will find those words written at the entrance to the hotel. The highest sense of hospitality is our founding principle.

The Connaught experience begins even before you walk through its door. It starts out front with *Silence*, a tranquil fountain designed by Japanese architect Tadao Ando. This is the first sign you are leaving the bustle of London's Mayfair behind. Step through the hotel's revolving door and you will find yourself enveloped in comfort. Deep carpets soften the sounds, dark wood relaxes the eyes and your eyes cannot help but be drawn to the famous staircase that spirals up to the guest rooms. If you look back at Mayfair through the windows, the outside world is truly a world away.

Such a magical atmosphere would not have the same allure without the Connaught's people though. Those wonderful individuals who unassumingly yet expertly guide you on an unforgettable journey, from the very first welcome through to each and every experience. It is thanks to these people that the Connaught has built an unparalleled hospitality, culinary and mixology legacy across its different outlets. Each one is unique in its genre, equally capable of blending timeless classicism with a bright and innovative spirit. Each one offers an inimitable experience for our guests.

Inside the Connaught you will find highly acclaimed restaurants, including Hélène Darroze at the Connaught, which has set new heights in the culinary arts and been awarded three Michelin stars; Jean-Georges at the Connaught, which invites guests to relax while enjoying the gastronomic delights crafted by world-famous chef Jean-Georges Vongerichten; and the newly reopened Connaught Grill, which brings you a modern interpretation of a 1960s steakhouse and provides an intimate and discreetly convivial experience. The hotel also contains several beautiful bars, including the world-famous Connaught Bar – of which more later; the Coburg Bar with its window onto Carlos Place, which makes it the perfect place to sit and people watch while you sip a coffee or a single-malt scotch; and the art-led Red Room, which focuses on the wines from the Connaught's enviable wine cellar. There's also an intimate cigar lounge and the Connaught Patisserie. Whatever you seek, the hotel fulfils your desires.

But what of the Connaught Bar? If you walk around the base of the staircase in the lobby, you will find a narrow corridor and a small reception desk in front of a pair of gold and darkened glass doors. Through those doors is the Connaught Bar, decorated in shades of soft gold, descending to dark, forest green leather. It is like looking deep into an ice-cold martini glass to see a perfect olive nestled below. There is no brashness in the décor. The bar's metal and crystal accents further this silvery image, evoking tumbling ice. In the Connaught Bar, as in the rest of the hotel, it is not the just the surroundings that make the experience; it is the warmth that emanates from the flawless service provided by the bar's team. You know from your first step into the bar that you are welcome and that it is here where you will be treated to the ultimate cocktail interlude.

Though I have come a long way from how I discerned flavours at the start of my bartending journey, my childhood continues to shape my taste and my standards of flavour. When I was a kid, we travelled every year to Puglia, in southern Italy, where my uncle maintained a piece of farmland. He grew tomatoes, olive trees, fig trees, watermelons – all sorts of traditional fruits and vegetables. Running around in the dusty red soil of those heat-baked fields and climbing trees to catch the summer breeze was my normality. So was working the harvest.

My heart still brims with the magic of those days: that sunlight, the air filled with fruity aromas, the sweetness of those tomatoes, the resin from the trees we climbed and that stuck on our hands – treasured in antiquity as myrrh. What I hadn't realized until recently is that my senses are still saturated with those memories. This charivari of flavours and aromas is so strongly rooted in me that it has become a sort of sixth sense.

It is this sense that guides me to discover new ingredients and to create new and different styles of drinks. It's this sense that tells me that something is authentic and delicious. Or not. And it's my childhood experiences and my Italian background that have set the foundation for my standards of flavour – the ones I apply to making cocktails.

While I could not possibly do what I do today without all the wisdom and brilliance of the people I have come across during my years as a mixologist, equally I could not do it without the sensory deluge of my childhood.

How did I arrive at the Connaught Bar? In 2006, I was working at Montgomery Place in London's Notting Hill district. One weekend a gentleman arrived for his usual Saturday brunch. This time he introduced himself and invited me to come to his bar for a Negroni. That was when I first encountered the dark, wood-panelled Connaught Bar thanks to Brian Silva, then its head bartender. At that time, I was on cloud nine. I had begun to travel the world doing presentations at bar shows and collaborating with Italian brands. I had a home base at Montgomery Place. I was happy with what I had. I was already very busy and was not seeking a new challenge, let alone a life-changing project. But serendipity has no limits.

There were only three American bars (bars where American-style drinks, more commonly known as cocktails, are served) in operation in London hotels at the end of 2006; they were at the Savoy, the Stafford and the Connaught. While a hotel has stood on Carlos Place since 1815, the Connaught came into existence in 1915 when the Coburg Hotel was renovated and re-christened. Grand and luxurious as it had been throughout the decades, the Connaught hotel's accommodations and facilities needed updating once again to flow with modern times. For this metamorphosis, the hotel closed in April 2007 and reopened in December that same year with only a few rooms, the Coburg Bar and the Gallery restaurant. The hotel management knew they wanted to preserve the traditional personality and heritage of this beautiful place – classic elegance with modern techniques to make the experience more comfortable for modern guests. The hotel's two bars would come to represent both aspects of the hotel itself: the Coburg Bar would salute the hotel's early classic years, while the Connaught Bar would embody modernity, shaking up the London bar scene but still standing the test of time.

Coming from his previous job managing the Blue Bar at the Berkeley Hotel, Santino Cicciari was brought on board as the Connaught's bar manager. He set about finding people who could bring something that didn't exist in other hotel bars. He approached me to head up bar operations for the Connaught Bar. I love a classic hotel bar: I experienced the bars at Duke's and the Dorchester as a guest when I first arrived in London. I also had experience in more casual bar atmospheres such as Salvatore and Amanda. But as much as I was fascinated by the style of service, by the elegance, by the attention to details, I didn't know if I could work with a large team – sixteen people – and the layers of management it takes to execute perfect cocktail service in a hotel setting. Santino helped me to realize this was more than a job, more than a promotion. It was my opportunity to put a different stamp onto what I do and to mature my own style.

It was perfect timing in many ways: the 2000s heralded the revival of classic cocktails and forgotten ingredients. Mixology was all about learning the stories behind those iconic drinks and the original ingredients used to make them. Dale DeGroff, Audrey Saunders, Gary Regan, Jared Brown, Anistatia Miller and Nick Strangeway were championing this cocktail renaissance and I got to meet all of them. They motivated me to dig deeper into history to stimulate my own creativity. It was the basic ethos from which we built the Connaught Bar's first concept: history with a twist, which you will see in many of the drinks in this book.

While the bar was being refurbished, I had one month to craft the Connaught Bar's opening menu. I was based in a tiny room with a refrigerator, a sink and Erik Lorincz, the senior bartender who was part of the opening team, working with me side by side. Inspired by classic cocktails that we researched in books scoured from old bookstores, we created The Connaught Martini, our own version of the Bloody Mary, Betty Is Back, Italian Job, La Lambada, Latina Daisy, and dozens of other drinks based on the work of classic bartenders such as Harry Craddock of the Savoy and William Tarling of the Café Royale as well as books written by 1930s journalist Charles H. Baker. The level of comfort achieved by offering something familiar but at the same time very fresh and new is what we accomplished for our guests.

We reinforced that relationship by giving a guest who loves a certain drink a printed copy of the recipe so they can revisit that experience at home, a custom we carry on to this day.

Many remarkable bartenders have honed their skills at the Connaught Bar since its 2008 opening. Each one contributed to the forging of the bar's culture before moving on to other great achievements. Erik Lorincz was part of the Connaught Bar's opening team before moving to the American Bar at the Savoy, and then on to his own Mayfair bar Kwãnt. Rusty Cerven inherited his position as senior mixologist, continuing the creative legacy, and Walter Pintus from 2015 to 2017 implemented a new layer of technicality and knowledge. Giorgio Bargiani arrived in 2014 as a barback (an assistant to the bartender) after having worked at The Hotel Splendido in Portofino and Le Manoir aux Quat'Saisons in Oxfordshire. He worked his way up to head mixologist and is now Assistant Director of Mixology. But our culture incorporates more than the talent behind the bar. There is the front of house to consider as well. Maura Milia first arrived in 2014, working as a cocktail waitress and then two years later as a supervisor. Her insights into how our drinks are served and what it takes to make a guest comfortable and enthusiastic about the experience have led her on a path to her current role as Bar Manager. It is this level of experience and insight that also directs our decision to develop and add a drink to a menu.

World travel, a love of photography, contemplation about emotions, sights and sounds, plus encountering a diverse range of guests help evolve our concept to include the visual nature of a drink's presentation and inspiration with ingredients from many countries and cultures. Introducing our guests to chicha morada from Peru, amaros from Italy, umeshu plum wine from Japan is our shared journey. We change our menu each year and continue to evolve what we present in subtle ways from these inspirations now that more and more of our team is involved in a collective way of thinking about the drinks we make and how we serve them. That includes me, as well as Maura and Giorgio, the bartenders, the front of house, the wait staff, the bar assistants, everyone. We have established a culture of mentoring our team and their successors. We believe that making drinks and serving drinks is a learning curve that never stops. Thus, we are at once teachers and eternal students. We gain knowledge by sharing. Our guests are the recipients of and testament to our collective approach.

As you peruse these pages, we hope you will find value and pleasure in the knowledge we at the Connaught Bar have learned. We hope you will savour your moments with these drinks as much as we have.

THE TOOLS OF THE CRAFT

Fine cocktail making has much in common with fine cuisine; only the best chefs know every nuance of every ingredient he or she moulds and shapes into a perfect masterpiece of gastronomy. With mixology, you need to know the heart and soul of your spirits and how to make the perfect accompaniments to share the stage. You must become a master of handling the tools that are the symbols of your craft as well as executing the best techniques for blending these components together, marrying aromas and flavours into the perfect equation. Finally, you need to know which vessel will serve as optimal presentation for your masterpiece, accentuating all the senses – sight, smell, taste, touch and sound. This chapter introduces you to the tools, techniques, glassware and spirits you will encounter in the recipes for this book. Together, these tools of the craft will accompany you on your path to making fine cocktails.

ESSENTIAL BAR TOOLS

Every good bartender needs a personal set of bar tools used to craft drinks. Here are the most important items to have on hand when setting up your home bar.

A MIXING GLASS is used for stirring drinks. It is designed with a pour spout and a wide opening that makes it easier to stir liquids and large ice cubes together. Alternatively, you can use a wide-mouthed pitcher, a large pint glass, a beer mug or a stein. A recent variation in the design of the mixing glass is the GALLONE. This large container lets you to stir a drink without using a barspoon. You simply swirl the gallone by holding it by the foot of the glass and moving it in a circular motion.

A COCKTAIL SHAKER is an important tool if you intend to shake or throw a drink. Throwing is a specific technique that consists of high pouring a liquid from the bigger piece of the Boston shaker filled with ice into the smaller one five or six times. The BOSTON SHAKER has one design consisting of two metal 'tins'. The other design pairs a glass vessel with a metal 'tin'. Both types can be used to shake or throw. The COBBLER SHAKER is a three-part shaker that alleviates the need for a strainer when pouring liquids into a glass. This design consists of a tin for the ingredients, a built-in strainer that fits over the tin and a cap that holds in the liquid while shaking.

There are three essential STRAINERS used in drink making. A HAWTHORN STRAINER is for straining shaken drinks from a Boston shaker. It is flat with a spring along the edge that fits snugly over the top of the shaker tin, allowing the liquid to flow through while pouring. A JULEP STRAINER is for straining stirred drinks from a mixing glass and for straining liquids while throwing a drink. A large spoon with holes rests on top of the ice in the mixing glass liquid to flow through while pouring. A FINE STRAINER is used to double strain a shaken drink to remove any small bits of ice, mint or fruit that escape from the Hawthorn strainer while pouring.

A BARSPOON for measuring and stirring is a long-handled metal spoon with a bowl that measures about 5 ml or 1 barspoon. There are three types of barspoons. The AMERICAN BARSPOON has a twisted handle and blunt cap opposite the bowl. The EUROPEAN BARSPOON has a flat crusher on the end opposite the bowl that is for lightly pressing mint or other solid ingredients in the mixing glass. The JAPANESE BARSPOON is heavier in weight and has a weighted teardrop opposite the bowl. A long metal spoon used for mixing iced tea will do.

A JIGGER is generally a two-sided vessel for measuring liquid. The large side – or jigger side – measures 44 ml (1.5 fl oz) of liquid. The small side – or pony side – measures 30 ml (1 fl oz). Another popular tool used by bartenders is the stainless-steel or copper-plated SPIRITS MEASURE. Stamped with its authorized CE capacity, these spirits measures are produced in a variety of sizes ranging from 25 ml (0.87 fl oz), 35 ml (1.18 fl oz), 40 ml (1.35 fl oz) and 50 ml (1.70 fl oz). The letters 'CE' signify that these are products traded on the extended Single Market in the European Economic Area (EEA) and have been assessed to meet high safety, health and environmental protection requirements. A SHOT GLASS can be used to measure. However, it is not as accurate for measuring outside of a jigger measure.

A VEGETABLE PEELER is the best tool for cutting thin twists of lemon, lime or orange. This tool is preferred by many bartenders because it is safer than a paring knife.

A MEXICAN ELBOW is a handheld citrus juicer that makes it easier to express juice without allowing the pips (seeds) to flow through.

ICE PRESSES or moulds are used to make ice spheres or diamonds. They are made from two pieces, one on top of the other, which are used to shape blocks of ice using weight and conductivity.

A DISC STAMP is a silcone mould with circular holes that can be filled to make unique garnishes.

A SMOKING GUN is a food and beverage smoker that is used to create smoke out of wood chips or dried herbs.

A small GLASS DECANTER is a small bottle with a capacity of 200 ml (7 fl oz).

Finally, a KNIFE and CHOPPING BOARD are indispensable for citrus wedges and wheels. Make sure you rinse your knife after every use. The acids from citrus dull the sharp edge very quickly.

As important as using the correct bar tools, knowing the appropriate glassware is like knowing to serve soup in a soup bowl or tea in a teacup. Here are some basic shapes along with a few options.

A CHAMPAGNE FLUTE is a narrow, medium-tall glass to serve champagne. It is fitted with an etched mark at the bottom of the glass that encourages and preserves the fizz in the drink. A CHAMPAGNE COUPE is a shallow, saucer-shaped glass commonly used for both champagne and cocktails. A COUPETTE is a smaller version of a champagne coupe, holding about 120 ml (4 fl oz) liquid and popular for serving cocktails.

A COCKTAIL GLASS, also called a MARTINI GLASS, is a classic V-shaped vessel used for serving many types of cocktails.

A COLLINS GLASS is a tall, narrow glass for serving 'long drinks' such as a Tom Collins or a gin and tonic. A HIGHBALL GLASS is a slightly shorter, wider version of the same style used for serving highballs – a category of drinks that contains a spirit and a mixer such as soda and ice. In a similar vein, a PILSNER GLASS is a tall, narrow glass that tapers to a short stem at the bottom. Traditionally, it is used to serve pilsner beer, but it makes a nice option for the collins or highball style. Finally, a KYOTO GLASS is a tall, narrow glass that tapers down to a flat base at the bottom.

The JULEP CUP takes its name from the drink traditionally made in this type of silver or silver-plated vessel, namely a julep. There are also modern versions fashioned from stainless steel or copperplate. This shape is also used when making a style of drink called a swizzle, in which ingredients are mixed with crushed ice without using a shaker or a mixing glass. Consequently, the exterior gets frosty cold when a drink is mixed inside. In a similar vein, the COPPER-PLATED MOSCOW MULE MUG can be used just like a julep cup.

A ROCKS GLASS takes its name from a nickname for ice. It is a short, broad vessel with a flat bottom. A rocks glass is sometimes called a TUMBLER or OLD FASHIONED GLASS, named after the popular drink served in this glass – the Old Fashioned. Rocks glasses vary in size from single to double capacity.

A WHITE WINE GLASS is an elegant, stemmed substitute for serving a drink that calls for a rocks glass or tumbler. A RED WINE GLASS is a stemmed glass with a bowl that is larger than a white wine glass and is a great substitute for serving highball drinks that include a spirit, mixer and ice.

There are nine basic mixing techniques that are very useful when making drinks at home. With a little practice, you can learn all of them in an evening.

CHILLING is an essential part of making a successful cocktail. You need to chill your glasses before you pour in your drink so the liquid doesn't warm too quickly. There are two ways to do this. The first method is to place your cocktail glasses or coupettes in the freezer until you are ready to pour your drinks, then take them out and add your drinks. Your finished creations will look and be frosty cold. The second method is to fill your cocktail glasses or coupettes with ice and water and let them stand while you mix your drinks. Ice alone will not chill them because the cold needs to come into complete contact with the glass. That's where the water comes in – to distribute the cold throughout the entire bowl of the glass. When ready, discard the ice and water, then add your drink.

STIRRING is an essential way to combine your ingredients, chill them and achieve the ideal dilution – the key to marrying your flavours. Fill a mixing glass halfway with ice cubes. If your ice is very cold and very hard, you need to stir your drink with a barspoon for about 30 seconds. If your ice is melty and soft, you need only stir for about 15 seconds. This is because you are trying to dilute the ingredients with water to about 25 per cent to achieve perfection.

BUILDING is the simplest way to make a drink. Place the individual ingredients directly into the glass in which it will be served, then add ice. To blend everything together, you can lift the ingredients with a spoon before you serve (see Lifting below).

LIFTING is the best way to mix a fizzy drink or one that contains a sparkling element. Do not stir the drink with a circular motion as you would if you were stirring. Reach the barspoon to the bottom of the glass and then lift it back out. You only need to do this once or twice to combine the ingredients while not losing your brilliant sparkle.

SHAKING is an art that is executed in two different ways for two different reasons. A SIMPLE SHAKE is used when there is no egg white or ice cream involved in making the drink. Fill the shaker about halfway with ice cubes and add the ingredients. Close the shaker firmly and grasp the top and bottom to ensure that the parts will not separate. Lift your shaker to about shoulder height and vigorously shake so you can feel the ice hitting the top and then the bottom of the shaker. While you shake, don't forget to smile. If you are using egg white in a drink, you need to do a DRY SHAKE without ice as your first step. Place your ingredients in the tin. Close the shaker, lift it up and vigorously shake so you can feel the ingredients shifting from the top to the bottom of the shaker. Then open the shaker and fill about halfway with ice cubes. Close the shaker and then do a HARD SHAKE – vigorously agitating the drink so you can hear the ice crashing from the top to the bottom of the shaker – to complete the process.

Although THROWING a drink sounds difficult, it is far easier than stirring and looks much fancier in front of your guests. Fill a shaker tin with ice cubes right to the top. Add your ingredients. Place a julep strainer over the ice. Holding the tin in one hand with a finger firmly placed on the strainer to keep it in place, raise the tin above your head. And hold an empty tin below in your other hand. Begin pouring from the full tin into the empty one. As you pour, lower the hand with the empty tin and let the liquid increasingly fall further before it is caught in the lower tin. Then bring the tins together and pour the liquid back into the tin over the julep strainer. Repeat three or four times. (To keep your shoes and floor dry, only watch the empty tin and never look at the tin above your head.)

Some drinks call for SWIZZLING, which requires either a swizzle stick or a barspoon. Build the ingredients for the drink in the serving glass. Fill the glass halfway with crushed ice. Submerge the horizontal prongs of the swizzle stick into the mixture and hold the shaft between your palms. Rapidly rotate the swizzle stick back and forth between your palms. When the glass appears well frosted, stop swizzling and add more crushed ice to the glass.

Most drinks, except for built drinks, need to be strained after mixing. There are two ways to STRAIN a drink. If you have stirred your drink, you can strain it by holding a julep or Hawthorn strainer firmly in the mixing glass to hold back the ice. Then, carefully pour the drink from the tin or shaker into the glass. If you have shaken your drink, you need to DOUBLE STRAIN it with a Hawthorn or julep strainer plus a fine strainer. After shaking the drink, place a Hawthorn strainer over the tin. Holding the two items firmly with one hand and a fine strainer in your other hand, pour the liquid through the fine strainer into the glass. Give the fine strainer an extra shake or two to get every drop of liquid into the glass.

CHAPTER

THE CONNAUGHT MARTINI

1

THE CONNAUGHT MARTINI

At once the simplest and most challenging of all cocktails, a Martini cocktail reveals the mixer's passion in every sip. At its best, the Martini transcends from mere cocktail to a concise and grand gesture that the work day is over, and the evening has begun. Anyone can make a Martini. Skill isn't required to combine gin and vermouth in a glass. But to make a great Martini cocktail, even a better Martini cocktail than the one before, can be a lifelong pursuit.

Is the art in the proportions? It seems as if the measures are the starting point of any conversation about Martini mixing. Then comes the brands of gin, vodka and vermouth. Yes, great gin, vodka and vermouth are required. Yet there is so much more. One of the most important aspects of the best Martini cocktails is that they are personal expressions. They are as unique to the mixer as a painting is to an artist.

While most seasoned Martini cocktail drinkers tell the bartender exactly how they would like their Martini cocktail made, there is an adventurous group who put their faith and trust in the bartender. By saying, 'as you prefer', you taste the bartender's personality, the bartender's true talent. When I first came to London, I experienced Martini cocktails at the hands of the masters. Peter Dorelli at the Savoy, Salvatore Calabrese at 50 St. James, Alessandro Palazzi at Dukes, Giuliano Morandin at the Dorchester. These masters of effortless hospitality each had their own style. I wanted to create the same when I arrived at the Connaught Bar.

THE DRINKS TROLLEY	We prepare our Martini cocktails tableside because the Martini is arguably the most personal of all drinks served today. More than simply mixing, we prefer to take our guests on a journey to flavour perfection.

Our trolley is essentially a simple portable bar, and far from a new concept. Although drink trolleys were used back in the late 1800s, they exploded onto the scene when Prohibition was repealed in the United States in the 1930s. Restaurants in New York were not allowed to have bars that were visible to their guests, because it was thought a visible bar would be an irresistible temptation to otherwise temperate diners. To circumvent this law, bartenders stepped out from behind their hidden bars, loaded service trolleys and mixed diners' drinks tableside. While this service style faded nearly into obscurity until the cocktail revival of the late 1990s and 2000s, we dearly love the added one-on-one time it affords us to spend with our guests. We keep a selection of guests' favourite gins and vodkas plus bottles of our house blend vermouth in the trolley's cabinet. On top are wells filled with olives and lemons as well as cocktail sticks (toothpicks). When a Connaught Martini is ordered, we go to the back of the bar to fill the mixing glass with ice and then we roll out the trolley, ready to perform.

THE BITTERS

The Martini cocktail is approaching its 140th birthday. Cocktail pioneer Harry Johnson added dashes of Boker's bitters and curaçao to his Martini cocktail recipe in 1888. More often than not, orange bitters were the preferred addition during the drink's first decades of popularity. Pedro Chicote, the father of modern Spanish bartending and author of many game-changing cocktail books in the 1920s and 1930s, enhanced his Martini cocktail with four dashes of Angostura Bitters. The truth is, the addition of bitters to this simple sip of gin and vermouth is the ideal place to add your personal touch, to create a Martini cocktail of your very own. Although most bars today omit the bitters, at the Connaught Bar we have created a series of bitters that allow us to personalize each Connaught Martini to our guests' palates.

We present this option on our drinks trolley. Five little dropper bottles of bespoke bitters are the key to our version of the Martini cocktail. Dr Ago's is a ginseng and bergamot bitters that is citrusy, woody and energizing. Dry lavender is both floral and calming with an aroma similar to rosemary and thyme. Coriander seeds impart a spicy, dark chocolate aroma that complements the botanicals in gin. Tonka bean blended with apricot kernels offers a sweet, woody aftertaste and provides a silky contrast to the gin's explosion of flavours. Black cardamom is both minty and citrusy, adding an extra touch of spice to the drink. How do you make the right choice? We have a business card-sized flavour mat printed with the names of each of the bitters. We place a drop of each in the appropriate square and let you smell each aroma. Then it is your choice which goes in and how much.

We gently pour about 2 ml or a scant ½ teaspoon of your chosen bitters using a dropper around the rim of a coupette. Because our bitters are diluted with spirit, they are not as intensely concentrated as an Angostura or other commercial bitters.

THE VERMOUTH	Our vermouth is a blend, not a single brand or style. We blend an extra dry vermouth, a dry floral vermouth and a bianco vermouth together to achieve the right balance of dryness, floral notes and a hint of chocolaty sweetness. I selected the three vermouths from the older and better-known brands. Piquepoul and catarratto, clairette blanche, and other thin, acidic wines that are the base for making vermouth give the perfect balance against either gin or vodka. The botanicals, led by the wormwood that gives vermouth its name, accent the wine. Interestingly, many vermouth botanicals – orange and lemon peel, liquorice root, cinnamon and cassia barks to name a few – mirror those in the gin and thus flawlessly accent it. But no matter which vermouth you choose to use, it is essential to remember that vermouth is hardly stronger than a red wine and lasts only a little longer before its fresh and complex notes fade, leaving it a bit soft and flabby. Once you open a bottle of vermouth, be sure to keep it in the refrigerator. It will last ten times longer when refrigerated.
THE ICE	The next important feature is the ice. The right kind of ice gives the drink a silky texture, something you do not get from tap water ice cubes. We used to make our own ice from filtered water through a long and slow freezing process with a house-made insulated container to ensure that the ice blocks were crystal clear. Because the Connaught Martini became extremely popular, we now have a commercial supplier that makes ice to our specifications. We fill a mixing glass about three-quarters full with clear ice.
THE GIN OR VODKA	Good gin makes a massive difference in a gin Martini cocktail. A good vodka does the same for a vodka Martini cocktail. Generally, we leave the choice of gin or vodka up to our guest, as well as the choice of which brand. The spotlight is on our guest's wishes not ours. We stir our Connaught Martinis in front of our guest. It's a big responsibility to stir such an important drink with precision – about 21 seconds – so it takes time before we let a new bartender who is properly trained and ready do this away from the bar. Using a Hawthorne strainer, we strain our Martini high above our head to give the drink some aeration as it falls into the glass and streams over the lemon twist (see below) to delicately express some of the fruit oils into the drink and to give the performance a little bit of dramatic flair.
THE OLIVE OR THE TWIST	If we use an olive, we spike it with three pinpricks to let a little of the juice run out into the glass, then we place it in the glass on a cocktail stick (toothpick). It is not a Dirty Martini, but it does allow some of the olive's aroma and flavour to join with the rest of the flavours in the drink. If we use a lemon twist, we use Amalfi lemons, which are delivered twice a week from Italy. (It is the same type of lemon that we use in its fresh state – not dried – in the distillation of our house-made Connaught Gin.) We use a vegetable peeler to carve a large piece of peel with the least amount of white pith. Combining this marriage of sights, sounds, flavours and aromas makes the experience of the Connaught Bar Martini both memorable and personal, worth revisiting more than once.

THE CONNAUGHT
MARTINI

DIFFICULTY [2]
ABV [3]
DRY

Whether it is the gin or vodka version, The Connaught Martini is an aromatized Martini that has been served following the same ritual since the day we opened the newly refurbished bar. It's a distillation of the Connaught Bar ethos – it's about approaching our guests. We want our new guests to get excited about what we do with our classic service, and we want our regular guests to feel comfortable and yet excited about trying something new.

2 ml (½ teaspoon) bitters of choice
15 ml (½ fl oz) vermouth blend
75 ml (2½ fl oz) gin or vodka of choice
Lemon twist or green olive

To make a martini with a twist: Using a dropper, gently pour the bitters around the rim of a frozen martini glass or coupette. Combine the vermouth and spirit in a mixing glass filled two-thirds with large ice cubes and stir until well chilled. Strain into the prepared martini glass, raising the mixing glass high to add aeration to the drink and squeezing the lemon twist into the drink as the liquid passes into the glass. Garnish with the lemon twist.

To make a martini with an olive: Using a dropper, gently pour the bitters around the rim of a frozen martini glass or coupette. Prick the olive three times with a cocktail stick (toothpick) and let a little juice run out into the glass. Combine the vermouth and spirit in a mixing glass filled two-thirds with large ice cubes and stir until well chilled. Strain into the prepared martini glass, raising the mixing glass high to add aeration to the drink. Garnish with the olive skewered onto the cocktail stick.

CHAPTER

100 CONNAUGHT BAR COCKTAILS

2

Creating moments of sensory delight through aroma, taste, sight and sound – this is the art of mixology. The perfect first impression takes a blend of the finest ingredients and essential skills, plus a true desire to make that first sip a memorable one for all the senses. Properly executed, it is so much more than just making drinks. But this is the real job of the bartender. In the immortal words of bartender and author Gary Regan, the bartender's job is to ensure that people leave feeling better than when they first arrived.

Inspiration for our drinks comes from many sources. While the recipes in this book are arranged alphabetically, the ideas behind their creation can be divided into four foundational categories. The first takes a classic cocktail and gives it a twist that either modernizes it for contemporary tastes or introduces a change of spirit from the traditional formulation. The second demonstrates how we have been inspired to create new concoctions by keeping our eyes open to the world around us and trying new tastes that we find during our travels around the globe. The third are recipes that you can make ahead of time, lasting about a week if they are kept refrigerated. This not only offers you the opportunity to savour these drinks more than once but to serve two or more at a time. Last but not least, the fourth group offer ideas for making exciting, refreshing potions that contain no alcohol, for moments when you want to enjoy sophisticated flavours without the spirits.

These recipes require lots of different shapes of ice, such as ice spheres and ice balls. Different ice shapes provide different dilutions and affect the liquid in different ways. According to the final result we want to achieve we use different kinds of ice. For example, crushed ice melts faster than ice cubes, while a big ice block in the drink melts gradually, which then dilutes the liquid slowly keeping it very cold.

Making cocktails with the special touches that identify them as Connaught originals occasionally requires crafting 'custom' ingredients. You can find all the recipes for homemade ingredients and batched recipes on pages 230–245.

21ST CENTURY

DIFFICULTY [2]
ABV [2]
SOUR, CHOCOLATY

The 21st Century takes a cue from the classic 20th Century cocktail, which was created by bartender C. A. Tucker and featured in William J. Tarling's 1938 volume the *Café Royal Cocktail Book*. A blend of London dry gin, crème de cacao, fresh lemon juice and Kina Lillet – a more herbaceous predecessor to today's Lillet Blanc aperitif. We decided to twist this classic sip into a softer version of another classic, Harry Craddock's Corpse Reviver No. 2, which was featured in Craddock's 1930 cocktail compilation *The Savoy Cocktail Book*. Our version has a citrusy edge like the Corpse Reviver No. 2, but the chocolate notes combine with the hint of spice from the rye in the genever to make this a very special modern update.

Edible gold paint, to decorate the glass
50ml (1¾ fl oz) Cacao Nib-infused Genever (page 237)
20 ml (⅔ fl oz) fresh lemon juice
20 ml (⅔ fl oz) Sugar Syrup (page 245)
20 ml (⅔ fl oz) Lillet Blanc

Brush the base of a coupette with edible gold paint and set aside. Combine the genever, lemon juice, sugar syrup and Lillet Blanc in a cocktail shaker filled with ice and shake vigorously until the drink is sufficiently chilled. Double strain into the prepared coupette.

AMBER BLACK

DIFFICULTY ³
ABV ²
RICH, FLORAL

While the activated charcoal and coconut garnish provides a visual representation of our Amber Black's name and character, the fundamental contrast is the balance of the bold flavours of cachaça and mastiha against soft Riesling and jasmine. While complementary flavours are a usual approach in a drink's creation, sometimes opposites really do attract. And contrasting tastes highlight each other's virtues. Korerima pods, native to Ethiopia, are unrelated but so like cardamom pods that they are sometimes called Ethiopian or false cardamom. However, here we seek the pepperiness unique to them as well as their fruity and perfumed character. You might expect a smoky and heavy drink with the blackness, yet this drink is light, sweet and rich, taking your mind from visual expectation to a very different visceral delight.

Neutral spirit, for spraying the glass
Powdered coconut and activated charcoal powder, for dusting the glass and to garnish
45 ml (1½ fl oz) Coconut and Coffee-infused Cachaça (page 237)
10 ml (⅓ fl oz) Korerima Pod-infused Mastiha (page 238)
5 ml (1 barspoon) Riesling Verjus Cordial
10 ml (⅓ fl oz) jasmine liqueur
30 ml (1 fl oz) soda water, for topping

Spray one side of a white wine glass with a neutral spirit and dust the same side of it with powdered coconut and activated charcoal powder with the help of a powder decorating shaker. Set aside. Combine the cachaça, mastiha, cordial and liqueur in a mixing glass filled with ice and stir until well chilled. Strain into a white wine glass over a chunk of ice. Top with the soda water. Garnish with powdered coconut and activated charcoal powder.

ANIMAE

DIFFICULTY ³
ABV ²
FRUITY, PEACHY

A mellow, sparkling blend of white peach and Prosecco with hints of grenadine and lemon juice, the ubiquitous Bellini was a seasonal sparkling cocktail introduced at Harry's Bar in Venice by the bar's owner Giuseppe Cipriani shortly after he opened for business in May 1931. But Cipriani didn't bother to name his special house aperitif until 1948, when a retrospective of Renaissance artist Giovanni Bellini was exhibited in the 'Floating City'. Our Animae pays tribute to this masterpiece in the art of sweet simplicity. It stirs animated feelings and emotions just like a fine painting, blending our house-made Clarified White Peach Purée (page 233) and Oat Liqueur (page 239) as the delicate enhancements in a vodka and champagne cocktail. But the soul of this drink is the garnish: a delicate peach sphere suspended in this crystal-clear cocktail. If you try to lift the sphere, you find you are piercing the Animae's soul.

20 ml (⅔ fl oz) vodka
10 ml (⅓ fl oz) Oat Liqueur (page 239)
30 ml (1 fl oz) Clarified White Peach Purée (page 233)
45 ml (1½ fl oz) champagne
Peach Sphere Water Cake (page 236), to garnish

Combine the vodka, liqueur, peach purée and champagne in a mixing glass filled with ice and stir until well chilled. Strain into a flute. Garnish with the water cake speared onto the end of a cocktail sword.

ASH CLOUD

DIFFICULTY ³
ABV ²
SOUR, SMOKY

When we created this drink, it was not so much a nod to the guests from the United States who were temporarily trapped in London by the eruption of the Icelandic volcano Eyjafjallajökull in 2010, but a dark twist on a favourite libation, the Paloma. While the original is a mix of blanco tequila, lime juice and grapefruit soda, our version adds sophisticated notes of fino sherry and washes the tequila with toasted sesame oil. The result is a toasty, subtly fruity sip that belies its spirituous nature.

45 ml (1½ fl oz) Toasted Sesame Oil-washed Blanco Tequila (page 234)
30 ml (1 fl oz) Grilled Grapefruit Sherbet (page 242)
10 ml (⅓ fl oz) fino sherry
10 ml (⅓ fl oz) fresh lime juice
Black Isomalt Disc Studded with Sesame Seeds (page 236), to garnish

Combine the tequila, sherbet, fino sherry and lime juice in a cocktail shaker filled with ice and shake vigorously until the drink is sufficiently chilled. Double strain into a coupette. Garnish with a black isomalt disc studded with sesame seeds.

ASTOR SPECIAL FIX

DIFFICULTY [2]
ABV [1]
FRUITY, HERBAL

Albert Stevens Crockett, historian of New York's old Waldorf-Astoria Hotel, questioned the origins of the Astor Cocktail. Was it a drink that was possibly created at the 'old Astor House or the Astor Hotel', and did it take its name 'from its bar of nativity'? Or was this blend of gin and Swedish Punsch (a bottled mixture of arrack, brandy or rum with lemon, spices, sugar and water) crafted to honour namesake William Waldorf Astor, who first built the Waldorf Hotel? Whatever the answers, the Astor was the hotel's signature cocktail after Waldorf's cousin John Jacob Astor IV built the adjacent Astor Hotel and the two buildings were united before the turn of the century to form the Waldorf-Astoria – the world's largest hotel at that time. Our version of the Astor is a special fix. While the classic drink consists of spirit, lemon juice and a sweet fruit, ours is more complex. It is made of wormwood-infused vodka, Matcha Syrup (page 244) and a touch of egg white, which makes it creamier in both palate and texture. The use of egg white to enrich the presentation with light foaminess as well as maraschino liqueur also harkens to another cocktail classic – the Ramos Gin Fizz.

50 ml (1¾ fl oz) wormwood-infused vodka
25 ml (¾ fl oz) fresh lemon juice
10 ml (⅓ fl oz) maraschino liqueur
20 ml (⅔ fl oz) Matcha Syrup (page 244)
15 ml (½ fl oz) egg white
50 ml (1¾ fl oz) soda water, for topping
Dried lime slices (see page 235), to garnish

Whizz the vodka, lemon juice, liqueur, syrup and egg white in a blender. Alternatively, you can dry shake these ingredients without ice in a cocktail shaker, then hard shake the mixture a second time in a cocktail shaker over ice. Double strain into a highball glass filled with ice. Top with the soda water and garnish with dried lime slices.

AVANT-GARDE

DIFFICULTY ³
ABV ²
BITTER, SOUR

Avant-garde: It is a word that encompasses the attributes of newness and experimentation in both conception and technique, especially in the worlds of art, music and literature. The essence of avant-garde can also be associated with the modern, forward-thinking movement seen in today's food and beverage world. Avant-garde is the mantra that drives the spirit of experimentation we present in every menu and every drink served at the Connaught Bar, and this libation is a tribute to this sentiment. The enigmatic Avant-Garde cocktail invites you to step between dimensions – from the historic to the exotic. Vodka is infused with barberries and mulberries. The striking purple hue and spicy notes come from our house-made Chicha Morada (page 232) – a Peruvian drink made from native purple corn, stone fruit and citrus spiced with cinnamon and cloves. On first sip, you notice that this drink is light on spirit, bright with fruitiness: clearly it is a drink that surprises you with hints of raspberry vinegar, vanilla-forward liqueur and lightly bitter amaro. Amaro Santoni is a liqueur made with thirty-four herbs. Its flavour is infused with undertones of citrus, olive leaves and iris and, above all, of rhubarb.

45 ml (1½ fl oz) Barberry and Mulberry-infused Vodka (page 238)
5 ml (1 barspoon) Amaro Santoni
30 ml (1 fl oz) Galliano l'Aperitivo
45 ml (1½ fl oz) Chicha Morada (page 232)

Combine the vodka, amaro, Galliano l'Aperitivo and chicha morada in a mixing glass filled ice and stir until well chilled. Strain into a coupette with a piece of block ice.

THE AVENUE

DIFFICULTY [1]
ABV [1]
SOUR, FLORAL

When the United Kingdom Bartenders' Guild was first organized in 1934, it was founded by two of London's top bartenders: Harry Craddock of the American Bar at the Savoy and William J. Tarling, who presided over the bar at the Café Royal off Piccadilly. Both gentlemen compiled the recipes being mixed at London's top bars. The Avenue appeared in Tarling's 1937 volume the *Café Royal Cocktail Book*. Originally crafted by G. Crompton, it was a blend of bourbon, Calvados – a French apple brandy – and passion fruit juice with dashes of grenadine and orange flower water. We came up with a modernized version that is insidiously fresh and rich in tropical fruitiness.

20 ml (⅔ fl oz) reposado tequila
30 ml (1 fl oz) bourbon
15 ml (½ fl oz) passion fruit purée
20 ml (⅔ fl oz) fresh orange juice
1 whole passion fruit, both pulp and seeds
10 ml (⅓ fl oz) Rosehip Syrup (page 245)
2 dashes orange flower water
½ passion fruit and edible flowers, to garnish

Combine the tequila, bourbon, passion fruit purée, orange juice, passion fruit pulp and seeds, syrup and orange flower water in a cocktail shaker filled with ice and shake vigorously until the drink is sufficiently chilled. Double strain into a coupette, then float the passion fruit on top and garnish with edible flowers.

BAMBOO

DIFFICULTY [3]
ABV [1]
DRY, RICH

Featured in the 1908 edition of *'Cocktail Bill' Boothby's World Drinks and How to Mix Them*, the original Bamboo is a sherry and sweet vermouth cocktail made famous by barman Louis Eppinger, who created the drink at his San Francisco bar on Halleck Street around the 1870s before he moved to Portland, Oregon, a decade later. His drink was already popular in the United States when he pulled up stakes and moved to Yokohama, Japan, where he managed the bar at the Grand Hotel and popularized his own creation among visiting American dignitaries and military personnel. This twist on the classic Bamboo was crafted by the team at the Connaught Bar in 2014. They modernized the recipe by reducing the sweetness, using a dry sherry and Coffee Bean-infused Extra Dry Vermouth (page 238) and introduced additional spiciness by combining orange bitters with the house ginseng-bergamot bitters. If you cannot find ginseng-bergamot bitters, blend equal parts of a bergamot liqueur with a gentian liqueur.

45 ml (1½ fl oz) oloroso sherry
45 ml (1½ fl oz) Coffee Bean-infused Extra Dry Vermouth (page 238)
2 dashes ginseng-bergamot bitters
2 dashes orange bitters
Orange twist, to garnish

Combine the sherry, vermouth and both bitters in a cocktail shaker filled with two-thirds ice and shake vigorously until the drink is sufficiently chilled. Double strain into a chilled coupette and garnish with a twist of orange.

A BEAUTIFUL MIND

DIFFICULTY [2]
ABV [1]
FRUITY, RESINOUS

It is a thing of beauty: A mind that is open to learning the new and different is likened to a blank canvas that is receptive to inspiration and vision. It is a blank canvas for creation, just like the young barbacks (assistants to the bartenders) and bartenders who come to work and learn with us. This drink is a fruity palate cleanser that is deceptively spirituous. The crispness of Polish vodka works with the tart, astringent flavour of the quince liqueur to balance the sweetness of both the Clarified Pineapple Juice (page 232) and the intensely sweet, pungent, balsamic aroma of Opopanax Syrup (page 245). Opopanax is the resin collected from the *Commiphora guidotti* tree, which is found in Africa and Asia. Sometimes this resin, which is used by perfumiers all over the world, is called sweet myrrh.

50 ml (1¾ fl oz) Polish vodka
10 ml (⅓ fl oz) quince liqueur
10 ml (⅓ fl oz) Opopanax Syrup (page 245)
45 ml (1½ fl oz) Clarified Pineapple Juice (page 232)
80 ml (2¾ fl oz) soda water
Dried pineapple slice (see page 235), to garnish

Combine the vodka, liqueur, syrup, juice and soda water in a mixing glass filled with ice and stir until well chilled. Strain into a highball glass filled with ice and garnish with a dried pineapple slice.

THE BENTLEY COCKTAIL

DIFFICULTY [1]
ABV [2]
SOUR, FRUITY

This take on a classic Bentley cocktail was crafted to celebrate the creation in 2016 of a new model Bentley automobile. The drink itself was made to be prepared in advance and served in the vehicle's little bar. If you cannot find ginseng-bergamot bitters, blend equal parts of a bergamot liqueur with a gentian liqueur.

50 ml (1¾ fl oz) single-cask whisky
20 ml (⅔ fl oz) fresh lemon juice
10 ml (⅓ fl oz) sloe gin
10 ml (⅓ fl oz) egg white
10 ml (⅓ fl oz) 30-year-old sherry
2 dashes ginseng-bergamot bitters
Carved lemon peel and a spray of green mandarin essence, to garnish

Combine the whisky, juice, sloe gin, egg white, sherry and bitters in a cocktail shaker and shake vigorously. Add enough ice to fill the shaker and hard shake. Double strain into a coupette and garnish with a carved lemon peel and a spray of green mandarin essence.

BENTLEY NO. 2

DIFFICULTY [1]
ABV [2]
FRUITY, WINEY

A Bentley Cocktail is among the treasure chest of drinks that Harry Craddock, head bartender of the American Bar at the Savoy, included in his 1930 *The Savoy Cocktail Book*. This blend of Calvados and a French aromatized wine, Dubonnet, inspired us to modernize the drink by adding an Asian touch: umeshu plum wine from Japan. The cherry and spice from the Peychaud's Bitters add an edge of complexity to this very simple and satisfying pre-dinner concoction.

45 ml (1½ fl oz) Calvados
30 ml (1 fl oz) umeshu plum wine
30 ml (1 fl oz) Dubonnet
2 dashes Peychaud's Bitters
Grapefruit twist, to garnish

Combine the Calvados, plum wine, Dubonnet and bitters in a mixing glass filled with ice and stir until well chilled. Strain into a coupette over a piece of block ice and garnish with a twist of grapefruit.

BENVENUTI

DIFFICULTY [2]
ABV [2]
FRUITY, MINTY

A warm smile and open arms followed by a cheerful '*benvenuti*!' greets friends, family and customers alike as the host welcomes all those who enter any door throughout Italy. This sparkling champagne cocktail celebrates the hospitality for which Italians are famed as well as the creation of a new 'Ambrato' style of vermouth di Torino, featuring floral and honeyed notes. With a fresh, herbaceous palate, this drink's gentle pineapple aroma mixes with the nepitella, which is also called lesser calamint – a mint that is traditionally cooked with mushrooms in Pisa, Italy. The result harkens to afternoons languishing on sunny dry hills overlooking a deep blue sea.

30 ml (1 fl oz) pineapple rum
20 ml (⅔ fl oz) Martini Riserva Speciale Ambrato
10 ml (⅓ fl oz) Nepitella Mint Syrup (page 244)
60 ml (2 fl oz) champagne
Diced pineapple piece, to garnish

Combine the rum, Ambrato and syrup in a cocktail shaker filled with ice and shake vigorously until the drink is sufficiently chilled. Double strain into a flute and slowly add the champagne. Garnish with a piece of diced pineapple speared onto the end of a cocktail sword, which replaces the bittered sugar cube usually found in traditional champagne cocktails.

BETTY IS BACK

DIFFICULTY [1]
ABV [1]
ACIDIC, FLORAL

'Betty is a joy ... she is far the best cocktail mixer in the West End', wrote a journalist in the 1940s about the Connaught Bar's head bartender. She first learned her skills working for twelve years behind the bar at the Hind's Hotel in Bray on Thames. With her well-honed talents she served Connaught Bar customers for fourteen years from the wartime years to a little beyond. This salute to Betty of the Connaught was the very first drink to appear on the refurbished Connaught Bar's opening menu. Regular customers from when the doors reopened in 2008 love it so much they keep requesting it. Betty is Back is a dry, bubbly sip with delicate floral and citrus notes from a complex blend of Aperol – an orange, gentian, rhubarb and cinchona aperitif – and elderflower liqueurs and fresh lemon juice, while the champagne raises a toast to this memorable wartime bartender and her customers, who kept returning to this iconic spot for more.

15 ml (½ fl oz) Aperol
5 ml (1 barspoon) elderflower liqueur
5 ml (1 barspoon) fresh lemon juice
100 ml (3½ fl oz) champagne
Cocktail cherry, to garnish

Combine the Aperol, liqueur and lemon juice in a mixing glass filled with ice and stir until well chilled. Strain into a flute and gently pour in the champagne. Garnish with a cocktail cherry speared onto the end of a cocktail sword.

BLACK L'ORBE

DIFFICULTY [1]
ABV [2]
SAVOURY, CHOCOLATY

This drink is dark and deceptive. It is made like a classic Vodka Martini but delivers so much more to the nose and palate. The stripe of black edible paint on the bowl of the glass sets the stage for this concoction of caviar vodka and crème de cacao with elegant notes of sherry, Calvados and Cocchi Americano, a wine-based aperitif that is aromatized with herbs and spices. Served with a wedge of salty cheese such as feta, Edam or Roquefort, this cocktail delights and surprises in its universe of the unexpected.

Edible black paint, to decorate the glass
30 ml (1 fl oz) caviar vodka
30 ml (1 fl oz) Cocchi Americano
15 ml (½ fl oz) dry sherry
10 ml (⅓ fl oz) crème de cacao
7.5 ml (¼ fl oz) Calvados

Paint a coupette with a streak of black edible paint and set aside. Combine the vodka, Cocchi Americano, dry sherry, crème de cacao and Calvados in a mixing glass filled with ice and stir until well chilled. Strain into the prepared coupette.

BLOODY MARY

DIFFICULTY [3]
ABV [1]
SAVOURY, RICH

A classic cocktail enjoyed before a meal, savoured before a Sunday brunch or on its own, the Bloody Mary was originally created by bartender Ferdinand 'Pete' Petiot and named by jazz pianist Ray Barton around 1920 at Harry's New York Bar in Paris. While the mixture was initially a simple blend of vodka and French tomato juice, it evolved over the decades when spicy elements such as Worcestershire, Tabasco and horseradish sauces were included in the repertoire. The celery stalk was added in 1966 at the Pump Room bar in Chicago's Ambassador East Hotel. But we started a new tradition by finishing our Bloody Mary with a Celery Air (page 235) that adds another layer of texture and freshness to a timeless classic.

10 ml (⅓ fl oz) fresh lemon juice
100 ml (3½ fl oz) tomato juice (if using American tomato juice, add a pinch of sugar to sweeten the juice)
20 ml (⅔ fl oz) Bloody Mary Mix (page 241)
50 ml (1¾ fl oz) gin, vodka or tequila
Celery Air (page 235) and a grating of nutmeg, to garnish

Pour the lemon and tomato juices, Bloody Mary mix and spirit into a cocktail shaker tin. Pour the mixture back and forth from the filled shaker to an empty shaker two or three times. Strain into a coupette without ice and top with celery air and a grating of nutmeg.

BLOSSOM ON THE BRANCH

DIFFICULTY [3]
ABV [1]
FLORAL, SOUR

Light as a blossom on a breeze, the Blossom on the Branch cocktail is overflowing with sensory aromas that are as fresh and rejuvenating as a walk through an orchard in bloom. This drink evokes images of sakura or cherry blossom season in Japan, when everyone picnics under cherry trees across the nation, toasting under the falling petals. Make sure that you buy the fresh jasmine blossom from food suppliers so it is food-safe before using it to garnish the drink.

30 ml (1 fl oz) pisco
40 ml (1⅓ fl oz) Tamarillo and Tea-infused Kombucha (page 237)
10 ml (⅓ fl oz) elderflower liqueur
Umeshu Sorbet (page 243)
Fresh jasmine blossom, to garnish

Combine the pisco, kombucha, liqueur and sorbet in a cocktail shaker filled with ice and shake vigorously until the drink is chilled. Strain into a wooden tumbler over ice chunks and garnish with jasmine blossom.

BRILLIANCE

DIFFICULTY [3]
ABV [1]
FRUITY, HERBAL

'You turn the corner. What a change! All is light and brilliancy.' That is how author Charles Dickens described the experience of walking into a drinking establishment in his 1833 story collection *Sketches by Boz*. It is a scene that is played out every day at the Connaught Bar. We were inspired by the mirror that presides over the actual bar, illuminating the magic performed as each drink is masterfully crafted. We were also inspired by a modern classic created by legendary American bar woman Audrey Saunders – The Old Cuban. (Think of a Mojito transformed into a champagne cocktail.) Our lighter, aromatic twist on this modern classic serves up fleeting impressions of coconut and extravagant spices such as saffron and *hoja santa*, which is also called Mexican pepperleaf or root beer plant. The overall impression is one of an exotically delicate Swiss lemon cream delight finished with a touch of sparkle.

40 ml (1⅓ fl oz) Coconut Oil-washed Puerto Rican Rum (page 233)
10 ml (⅓ fl oz) young, blended rhum agricole
10 ml (⅓ fl oz) Bénédictine
10 ml (⅓ fl oz) Hoja Santa and Saffron Syrup (page 244)
60 ml (2 fl oz) champagne
White chocolate disc with a single hole, to garnish

Combine the rum, rhum agricole, Bénédictine, syrup and champagne in a mixing glass filled with ice and stir until well chilled. Strain into a white wine glass filled with ice and garnish with a white chocolate disc with a single hole.

BUBBLE LEAF

DIFFICULTY [3]
ABV [1]
FRUITY, LEMONY

When I first arrived at the Connaught Bar in 2008, I was inspired to craft an Italian twist on a staple in the Connaught Bar's drink menu – the French 75. While many historians say this Parisian classic was invented by Harry MacElhone during the 1920s at the New York Bar, Robert Vermiere told a different story in his 1922 volume *Cocktails: How to Mix Them*. He wrote that the French 75 was introduced by bartender Henry Tépé at Henry's Hotel on Rue de Volney, which was frequented by American ambulance drivers and aviators during the First World War. But when Henry died suddenly, Harry took up the mantle and popularized the drink at his place. Many versions have dictated champagne was the bubbly in the French 75. But I agree with the late Sasha Petraske of Milk & Honey in New York that the drink can sparkle with cava, Prosecco or other sparkling wine. The Bubble Leaf contains two very refreshing twists: the acidity of ice wine verjus (a highly acidic juice pressed from grapes or other sour fruit) plus the fruity sparkle of Italian apple and pear cider.

50 ml (1¾ fl oz) aromatic, floral gin
20 ml (⅔ fl oz) ice wine verjus
20 ml (⅔ fl oz) Amalfi Lemon Leaf Syrup (page 244)
45 ml (1½ fl oz) Italian apple and pear cider
Lemon leaf essence and a cocktail cherry, to garnish

Combine the gin, verjus and syrup in a cocktail shaker filled with ice and shake vigorously until the drink is sufficiently chilled. Double strain into a flute and top with the cider. Garnish with a spray of lemon leaf essence and a cocktail cherry skewered onto a wooden stick.

BUMBLEBEE

DIFFICULTY [2]
ABV [2]
FRUITY, RICH

The roly-poly, fuzzy members of the bee family – bumblebees – seem to love a leisurely graze through the countryside's bounty of flowers, coaxing them to bear the luscious berries we harvest from hedgerow to hedgerow. This Bumblebee is a twist on a modern classic – The Bramble. It has a dry, deep fruit texture but is not as fruity as its predecessor. The addition of champagne to this elegant gin cocktail lightens its berry richness with hints of toast and apple, with just the right amount of sparkle. Fat-washing (infusing alcohol with oily or fatty ingredients) vodka and gin in a mixture of berries, olive oil, salt and pepper makes this creation a salute to the hedgerows and the shepherds of the fruit harvest – the bumblebees.

45 ml (1½ fl oz) Berry and Grapeseed Oil-washed Vodka and Gin (page 234)
5 ml (1 barspoon) concord grape vinegar
5 ml (1 barspoon) Sugar Syrup (page 245)
50 ml (1¾ fl oz) champagne
Blackberry half, to garnish

Place a piece of ice into a coupette. Combine the vodka, vinegar and sugar syrup in a mixing glass filled with ice and stir until well chilled. Strain the mixture into the coupette and gently add the champagne. Garnish with a blackberry half set on top of an ice cube.

BURNING PEAT

DIFFICULTY ²
ABV ²
RICH, MALTY

This drink appeared in our Ignis series of drinks that were inspired by the element of fire. Smoky, spicy and daring, these cocktails have walked across hot embers to get here, their components burnt or roasted to conjure the heat and drama of fire. The sherry contributes to the character imbued by the best ageing barrels. The barley tea provides another dimension: the grain that makes whisky so distinctive. Oleo saccharum is a technique of extracting citrus oil, mainly lemon, into sugar. Citrus rinds are mixed with a lot of sugar and left to stand to extract all the oils, resulting in a sweet, fruity syrup. It was used by nineteenth-century bartenders to give a drink citrus and sweetness. Our house-made Oleo Saccharum Citrus Sugar (page 243) is made with orange peel instead of lemon.

45 ml (1½ fl oz) 18-year-old blended whisky
5 ml (1 barspoon) 16-year-old Islay whisky
10 ml (⅓ fl oz) dry sherry
90 ml (3 fl oz) brewed barley tea
10 ml (⅓ fl oz) Oleo Saccharum Citrus Sugar (page 244)
Crunchy Barley Sponge (page 235), to garnish

Combine the whiskies, sherry, barley tea and sugar in a cocktail shaker filled with ice and shake vigorously until the drink is sufficiently chilled. Strain into a silver mug with crushed ice and garnish with a crunchy barley sponge.

CAVIAR MARTINI

DIFFICULTY [1]
ABV [3]
SAVOURY, DRY

Remember we said vodka accentuates any flavour it encounters?
Well, caviar vodka is a niche spirit that has entered the spirits pantheon.
It accentuates caviar's 'breath of the sea' aroma with a richer palate
than that of oysters coupled with hits of nuttiness and saltiness. Its high
minerality complements the butteriness of lush Puligny-Montrachet
wine that replaces the traditional vermouth element in a Martini.
The pairing of these exquisite ingredients makes this a very elegant drink.
We recommend an accompaniment of a small dish of Japanese wakame
seaweed or sashimi, such as sea bream garnished with toasted nori.

50 ml (1¾ fl oz) caviar vodka
20 ml (⅔ fl oz) Puligny-Montrachet wine
15 ml (½ fl oz) dry sherry
2 dashes tonka bitters (see page 256)
Piece of pickled beetroot or a cocktail onion, to garnish

Combine the vodka, wine, sherry and bitters in a mixing glass filled
with ice and stir until well chilled. Strain into a chilled cocktail glass and
garnish with a piece of pickled beetroot or a cocktail onion speared
onto the end of a cocktail pick.

CHATHAM SPECIAL

DIFFICULTY [3]
ABV [1]
MILKY, SPICY

It's easy to get the Chatham Hotel Special mixed up with the Chatham Special. While the Chatham Cocktail's true origins remain undiscovered at this time (sometimes attributed to the Chatham Hotel in New York), the libation of gin, ginger brandy and lemon appeared on Macy's department store luncheon menus in 1913 and 1914 and today it remains an essential and influential if rare drink. But the Chatham Special was a horse of another colour, invented by Felix Cotto at the Chatham Hotel in Paris. He entered his creation in a 1950 'World Competition' according to bartender-author Eddie Clark in his 1954 book *King Cocktail: Shake Again with Eddie*. Cotto's Chatham Special was structured with rum, lemon juice and pineapple syrup; our Chatham Special has a similar profile but is made with profoundly Connaught Bar-style ingredients.

Neutral spirit, for spraying the glass
Cocoa powder, for dusting the glass
30 ml (1 fl oz) cognac
20 ml (⅔ fl oz) Earl Grey Tea-infused Port Wine (page 239)
10 ml (⅓ fl oz) Amaro Lucano
20 ml (⅔ fl oz) Spiced Rice Milk (page 243)
Tonka bean (see page 256) and a spice bag filled with some cinnamon sticks and cloves, to garnish

Spray the exterior of a coupette with a neutral spirit and dust the exterior with cocoa powder with the help of a powder decorating shaker. Set aside. Shake the cognac, wine, amaro and rice milk in a cocktail shaker over ice. Double strain into the prepared coupette and garnish with grated tonka bean and the spice bag tied onto a stirring stick and suspended over the edge of the glass.

CHEEK TO CHEEK

DIFFICULTY [1]
ABV [2]
SOUR, ORANGEY

A classic that sits alongside the Martini and the Manhattan, The Sidecar is a timeless creation with enigmatic origins, just like its siblings. This cognac, curaçao triple sec and lemon juice masterpiece appeared in two books in 1922: Robert Vermeire's *Cocktails: How to Mix Them* and Harry MacElhone's *Harry's ABC of Mixing Cocktails*. Who was its creator? MacElhone claimed it was Malachi 'Pat' McGarry at the Buck's Club. Vermeire said it was born at the Carlton Hotel in Cannes. Our twist on this simple masterpiece replaces the lemon juice with the high acidity of verjus. The drops of ginseng-bergamot bitters impart more complexity. If you cannot find ginseng-bergamot bitters, blend equal parts of a bergamot liqueur with a gentian liqueur. The touch of honey blended with equal parts of water to make it mixable imparts a sophisticated sweetness that makes our Cheek to Cheek a distinctive descendant.

45 ml (1½ fl oz) cognac
15 ml (½ fl oz) curaçao triple sec
20 ml (⅔ fl oz) verjus (verjuice)
10 ml (⅓ fl oz) honey-water (1 teaspoon honey and 1 teaspoon still mineral water mixed together)
Drops of ginseng-bergamot bitters
Lemon twist, to garnish

Combine the cognac, triple sec, verjus and honey-water in a mixing glass filled with ice and stir until well chilled. Add a couple of drops of bitters into the bottom of a coupette. Strain the contents of the shaker into the coupette and garnish with a lemon twist.

CHILL OUT

DIFFICULTY [1]
ABV NA
FRUITY, PIQUANT

Relaxation is truly a state of mind, and chillies have been documented to offer us a way to achieve it. The secret to finding peace is simply to accept it – to chill out. In this Chill Out, the balance of sweet, citrus, spice and dilution is an essential structure for a non-alcoholic drink. Here, the orange and lemon are balanced by the syrup yet accentuated by the chilli, while the passion fruit brings softness and a distinctive taste of the tropics. It is the perfect drink when you want to chill out if you're not drinking or wish to set a slower pace for the evening.

35 ml (1¼ fl oz) fresh orange juice
20 ml (⅔ fl oz) fresh lemon juice
20 ml (⅔ fl oz) Chilli Syrup (page 244)
15 ml (½ fl oz) passion fruit purée
1 whole passion fruit, both pulp and seeds
½ passion fruit and a dried chilli, to garnish

Combine the orange and lemon juices, syrup, purée and passion fruit pulp and seeds in a cocktail shaker filled with ice and shake vigorously until the drink is sufficiently chilled. Double strain into a white wine glass over a piece of block ice. Garnish with the passion fruit and dried chilli.

CITRUS VIBE

DIFFICULTY [2]
ABV NA
SOUR, SPICY

Say, 'It's the vibe' to pretty much any Australian and they might reply, 'Tell him he's dreaming' or 'How's the serenity? So much serenity.' If you haven't seen the 1997 movie *The Castle*, it's a feelgood comedy that defines their nation. Combining fresh orange juice, Spicy Calamansi Sherbet (page 242), orgeat (an almond syrup enhanced with flower water) and ginger beer, Citrus Vibe is delicious – a non-alcoholic Mai Tai ready to whisk you away to … Bonnie Doon, the serene holiday destination in *The Castle*.

50 ml (1¾ fl oz) fresh orange juice
30 ml (1 fl oz) Spicy Calamansi Sherbet (page 242)
10 ml (⅓ fl oz) orgeat
30 ml (1 fl oz) ginger beer
Edible flowers and ground cinnamon, to garnish

Combine the juice, sherbet, orgeat and ginger beer in a mixing glass filled with ice and stir until well chilled. Strain into a white wine glass filled with ice and garnish with edible flowers and a sprinkle of ground cinnamon.

CLOUD NINE

DIFFICULTY ³
ABV ²
CITRUSY, FRUITY

When you say you are on 'cloud nine' you mean you are experiencing a feeling of well-being or elation. Essentially, this drink is a classic whiskey sour made with rich, sweet bourbon that is complemented with our house-made Pistachio and Raspberry Milk (page 239). Surprising notes of nuttiness and fruitiness balance against the Cocchi Americano infusion that highlights both the citrus and the brightness of the Szechuan pepper. Soft and approachable, this heaven-sent whiskey creation is topped with an ethereal foam made with Miraculous Foamer, a plant-based liquid used to replace egg white in a drink. You can use pasteurized egg white as an alternative, but you will need to dry shake the bourbon, milk and vermouth and then hard shake with ice. Either way you mix this creation, it is boundless joy in liquid form.

50 ml (1¾ fl oz) bourbon
20 ml (⅔ fl oz) Pistachio and Raspberry Milk (page 239)
20 ml (⅔ fl oz) Orange, Clementine and Szechuan Pepper-infused Cocchi Americano (page 237)
Dash of Miraculous Foamer
Blue spirulina liquid, to garnish

Combine the bourbon, milk and Cocchi Americano in a cocktail shaker filled with ice cubes and shake vigorously until the drink is sufficiently chilled. Strain into a coupette. Top with Miraculous Foamer. Finally, spray blue spirulina liquid (a protein extracted from blue-green algae) over the top to make a cloud-like effect and use a spoon to create a spiral on the surface of the foam.

COOPERSTOWN JULEP

DIFFICULTY [2]
ABV [1]
HERBAL, ORANGEY

Albert Stevens Crockett, historian of New York's old Waldorf-Astoria Hotel, noted in his 1934 book *The Old Waldorf-Astoria Bar Book* that the Cooperstown cocktail was a 'Bronx, with fresh mint'. Invented by the hotel's bartender Johnny Solon, this refreshing blend of gin, fresh orange juice, mint and dashes of both red and dry vermouths inspired our icy, summery treat, which deepens the relationship between the ingredients with the introduction of port. Fashioning this classic into a julep drink enhances the Cooperstown Julep's light and fruity character. It will make even the hottest day fly by on a fresh breeze.

50 ml (1¾ fl oz) sencha dry gin
40 ml (1⅓ fl oz) LBV (late-bottled vintage) port
30 ml (1 fl oz) Orange and Honey Shrub (page 243)
6 fresh mint leaves
Mint sprigs and dried orange slices (see page 235), to garnish

Swizzle the gin, port, shrub and mint leaves in a julep cup with a little crushed ice. Add more crushed ice and garnish with mint sprigs and a couple of dried orange slices.

COPPER AND BLUE

DIFFICULTY [1]
ABV [1]
FRUITY, COCONUTY

The Copper and Blue is inspired by the image of Britons on holiday on the beach. This twist on a classic Piña Colada reflects a love for the tropical and for chilled white wine. There's a hint of elegance and of the exotic from the use of Martini Riserva Speciale Ambrato, a floral and honey-laced vermouth di Torino, plus Sancerre wine from the Loire valley in France, which make an otherwise simple mix of rum, pineapple and coconut into a previously uncharted tropical destination.

Neutral spirit, for spraying the glass
Copper-hued Powder (page 242), for dusting the glass and to garnish
100 ml (3½ fl oz) Copper and Blue Milk Punch (page 240)
10 ml (⅓ fl oz) Blue Sancerre Wine (page 245)

Spray one side of a white wine glass with a neutral spirit and dust the same side of it with copper-hued powder with the help of a powder decorating shaker. Set aside. Combine the milk punch and wine in a mixing glass filled with ice and stir until well chilled. Strain into a white wine glass over a piece of block ice and garnish with a sprinkle of copper-hued powder.

CORAL

DIFFICULTY [3]
ABV [2]
FRUITY, FLORAL

Like its namesake, this ruby-red cocktail is delicate, yet intricately structured with all its elements working together to form a unified whole. The Coral layers soft, sparkling strawberry and warming elderflower notes with a spirited kick of tequila and mescal. This drink may look fragile but in truth, it is very spirituous, with deceptive floral and spicy notes from our house-made Bee Balm and Cassia Cordial (page 233) plus the heat of the Giffard Espelette liqueur, a chilli liqueur produced on a *rhum agricole* base.

Edible coral paint, to decorate the glass
20 ml (⅔ fl oz) blanco tequila
10 ml (⅓ fl oz) mescal
10 ml (⅓ fl oz) elderflower liqueur
10 ml (⅓ fl oz) Giffard Espelette Liqueur
10 ml (⅓ fl oz) Bee Balm and Cassia Cordial (page 233)
100 ml (3½ fl oz) Sparkling Strawberry Wine (page 245)

Paint a tumbler or rocks glass with a stripe of coral-coloured edible paint and set aside. Combine the tequila, mescal, liqueurs, cordial and sparkling wine in a mixing glass filled with ice and stir until well chilled. Strain into the prepared tumbler.

DANDELION COCKTAIL

DIFFICULTY [3]
ABV [1]
CREAMY, BITTER

Dandelion coffee is a herbal tea made from roasted dandelion roots that is commonly served as a coffee substitute because it has the taste and appearance of coffee. We decided to infuse this deep, satisfying flavour into cognac and complement it with the nuttiness of cashew milk, the elegance of sherry and the sweetness of Salted Date Syrup (page 245). The grating of tonka beans (see page 256) adds a warm hint of vanilla. As an option, a sprinkle of mahlab – a Mediterranean spice made from St Lucy's cherry seeds – adds hints of cherry, rose, almond and vanilla.

Edible gold paint, to decorate the glass
40 ml (1⅓ fl oz) Dandelion Coffee-infused Cognac (page 237)
15 ml (½ fl oz) cashew milk
15 ml (½ fl oz) Salted Date Syrup (page 245)
10 ml (⅓ fl oz) oloroso sherry
Tonka bean (see page 256), for grating
Clear Isomalt Disc Studded with Pollen (page 236), to garnish

Paint a flute with a stripe of edible gold paint and set aside. Shake the cognac, cashew milk, syrup and sherry in a cocktail shaker filled with ice. Double strain into the prepared flute. Grate the tonka bean over the drink and garnish with a clear isomalt disc studded with pollen.

DAYDREAMING

DIFFICULTY [2]
ABV [2]
FRUITY, BITTER

What a beautiful day for a daydream! You know, every day is the ideal time in the week to muse and reflect, far from the stresses of the everyday world. Think of some happy moment that has already taken place or look into the future and plan how to make that moment a reality. When you daydream over a cocktail like our Daydreaming, it will whisk you away to a sunny place overlooking clear blue water. Its effervescent sparkle and deep rum notes dance along with hints of wine, herbs and spices to bring you to a happy spot at the end of a long workday.

40 ml (1⅓ fl oz) aged Dominican Republic rum
10 ml (⅓ fl oz) Amaro Santoni
10 ml (⅓ fl oz) Connaught Bar Sweet Vermouth Mix (page 241)
10 ml (⅓ fl oz) Bitters Mix (page 241)
15 ml (½ fl oz) sherry
30 ml (1 fl oz) champagne
10 ml (⅓ fl oz) Tropical Milk Jam (page 239)
Mango and Green Mandarin Leather Leaf (page 236), to garnish

Combine the rum, amaro, vermouth mix, bitters mix, sherry, champagne and milk jam in a mixing glass filled with ice and stir until well chilled. Strain into a red wine glass fitted with a chunk of ice and garnish with a mango and green mandarin leather leaf.

THE DUSK

DIFFICULTY ²
ABV ²
SOUR, FRUITY

It is sunset. The light softens and the Connaught Bar is transformed. The Dusk is luminosity in a glass. Passion fruit and grapefruit notes are crowned by a delicate sunset, capturing the bar's shift from day to evening – the magic hour when the bar springs to life. A very light, very approachable drink, The Dusk has a hint of a fernet-style amaro spiciness – a popular bitter aromatic Italian spirit served as a digestif. Passion berries are unrelated to passion fruit, yet they convey similar and complementary flavours and work beautifully together, and both match flawlessly with the buttery, grassy notes of the tequila. If you can't get grapefruit and hops bitters, use grapefruit bitters instead.

50 ml (1¾ fl oz) Passion Fruit and Passion Berry Milk (page 239)
40 ml (1⅓ fl oz) reposado tequila
5 ml (1 barspoon) vetiver liqueur
5 ml (1 barspoon) grapefruit and hops bitters
Clear Isomalt Disc (page 236), to garnish

Combine the milk, tequila, liqueur and bitters in a mixing glass filled with ice and stir until well chilled. Fill a Kyoto glass with ice cubes. Strain the drink into the glass and garnish with a clear isomalt disc.

ECHO

DIFFICULTY ³
ABV NA
FRUITY, WOODY

Echoes reverberate in both the senses and the soul. Our Echo resounds with the colours, flavours and aromas of a Negroni, while presenting its softer, non-alcoholic side. It is made with Martini Vibrante – a citrusy, red non-alcoholic Italian aperitif. Expressing the traditional bittersweet palette of herbal, fruity and gently spiced notes, this libation is a new Italian classic aperitif in the making.

50 ml (1¾ fl oz) Martini Vibrante
30 ml (1 fl oz) Clarified White Peach Purée (page 233)
20 ml (⅔ fl oz) Bee Balm and Cassia Cordial (page 233)
Small white chocolate disc and large white chocolate disc, to garnish

Combine the Martini Vibrante, peach purée and cordial in a mixing glass filled with ice and stir until well chilled. Strain into a coupette with a piece of block ice and garnish with a small white chocolate disc and a large white chocolate disc on the ice block.

ECLIPSE

DIFFICULTY [3]
ABV [1]
BITTER, CHOCOLATY

Throughout history, an eclipse has been regarded as a remarkable visual event that challenges and exhilarates the senses as the passage of one celestial body obscures the light of another in the sky. When a solar eclipse occurs, the sun is haloed by its own rays while its centre appears blackened out. When Giorgio and I collaborated on the presentation of this drink with our good friend, the photographer Alan Schaller, we wanted to emulate that experience. The result: a crystal tumbler that is white on the outside and glazed black on the inside. By obscuring the sipper's sight of the liquid, their other senses are heightened, including imagination. The flavours of gin, vermouth, amaro and cocoa may seem familiar but the surprise hints of Japanese botanicals and 'new make' wine (a wine that comes from the first fermentation of grape juice and has not been aged after fermentation) transform this experience into a very special moment. Spice and wood notes predominate the profile with a light citrusy finish in this playful game that excites the senses just like an eclipse of the sun.

30 ml (1 fl oz) Japanese gin
60 ml (2 fl oz) Eclipse Pre-mix (page 241)
10 ml (⅓ fl oz) new make wine

Combine the gin, pre-mix and wine in a mixing glass filled with ice. Stir and strain into a crystal tumbler half-filled with cracked ice.

ELLIPSIS

DIFFICULTY [2]
ABV [1]
MILKY, CITRUSY

An ellipsis is a pause that you take from the choices you need to make in life. The pause you make with us is an ellipsis in your day. This drink celebrates customers who choose to take their break during a hectic, frazzling day with us at the Connaught Bar.

60 ml (2 fl oz) Ellipsis Milk Punch (page 240)
30 ml (1 fl oz) kombucha
Edible blue paint, to garnish

Combine the milk punch and kombucha in a mixing glass filled with ice and stir until well chilled. Strain into a rocks glass or a tumbler with a piece of block ice. Garnish with three dots of edible blue paint on the ice block.

EVERGLOW

DIFFICULTY ³
ABV ³
BITTER, NUTTY

A feeling of warmth and happiness – an everglow – is a fleeting sensation suspended in time. In the subdued lights of the Connaught Bar, the faces of our customers glow in the soft warmth. This feminine variation of a classic Manhattan is a timeless homage to the lightness, the darkness and the space that melds in between them. The enveloping russet hues of rich rum and rye infused with wattleseeds from the Australian acacia tree augment the bright glimmer of the blackberries infused into the red vermouth and the nuttiness of the eau de noix, a walnut -infused liqueur. The intricacies of aromas and flavours in this rich, complex blend are best complemented with a piece of Parlick Fell or other light, sheep's milk cheese.

30 ml (1 fl oz) Wattleseed-infused Venezuelan-style Rum (page 238)
20 ml (⅔ fl oz) Wattleseed-infused Rye (page 238)
20 ml (⅔ fl oz) Blackberry-infused Sweet Vermouth (page 238)
5 ml (1 barspoon) artichoke amaro
20 ml (⅔ fl oz) eau de noix
White chocolate disc, to garnish

Combine the rum, rye, vermouth, amaro and eau de noix in a mixing glass filled with ice and stir until well chilled. Strain into an old fashioned glass or a tumbler with a piece of block ice and garnish with a disc of white chocolate on the ice block.

FARAWAY COLLINS

DIFFICULTY [3]
ABV [1]
SOUR, SPICY

The long and refreshing Faraway Collins was created in 2012 to encompass the familiar flavours and aromas of London and the faraway destinations of Japan, Australia and Mexico. It began its journey as a drink known simply as the Collins, which was invented in eighteenth-century London. The Collins was originally made with a spirit, such as gin or whisky, sugar, lemon juice and carbonated water (seltzer) – another invention that was introduced in the British capital during the 1790s. The Faraway Collins then heads eastward, stopping in Japan to meet the juice of the yuzu: a fruit that combines the strong citrus of lemon with the heady floral notes of wild mandarin oranges and a delicate lime blossom aroma. Journeying south to Australia, it acquires its aromatic sweetness from our house-made Eucalyptus Syrup (page 244), which imparts the cooling sensations of menthol, citrus and pine. Finally, this refreshing cocktail meets the intensely root beer-like qualities of Sarsaparilla-infused Soda Water (page 238), with its hints of wintergreen, liquorice, black cherry bark, sweet birch and cinnamon. When it returns homeward from its journey, the Faraway Collins offers a deep palate and even deeper texture to a refreshingly familiar English summertime classic. Besides being a perfect garden party drink, it pairs well with grilled (broiled) chicken skewers or a light fish, such as cod, Dover sole or sea bass.

50 ml (1¾ fl oz) London dry gin
20 ml (⅔ fl oz) Eucalyptus Syrup (page 244)
20 ml (⅔ fl oz) Yuzu Juice (page 235)
100 ml (3½ fl oz) Sarsaparilla-infused Soda Water (page 238)
Dried eucalyptus leaves, a lemon twist and a dried half Persian lime (see page 235), to garnish

Gently swirl the gin, syrup, yuzu juice and soda water in a gallone mixing glass over ice cubes. Strain into a highball glass filled with ice and garnish with dried eucalyptus leaves, a lemon twist and a dried half Persian lime.

FLEURISSIMO

DIFFICULTY [1]
ABV [2]
FLORAL, SPICY

This elegant twist on a classic champagne cocktail was created in honour of Connaught hotel guest Princess Grace of Monaco. Named after the signature floral fragrance crafted for the princess's 1956 wedding by perfumer James Henry Creed, the Fleurissimo has a special bouquet of floral notes, highlighted by violets. It is the subtle aroma of Parma violets – the distinctively aromatic, deep purple flowers used to make both a popular British sweet (candy) as well as crème de violette liqueur – that ennobles this cocktail. The first sip delivers a delicate surprise as notes of cherry, clove and nutmeg from the Peychaud's Bitters complement the toasty, effervescence of the main attraction, the champagne. A soft, floral experience, the Fleurissimo is a regular feature on the Connaught Bar menu. It works well as an aperitif with a small dish of salty nibbles, such as nuts and crisps (potato chips), or as an overture to sushi.

1 sugar cube
2 dashes Peychaud's Bitters
5 ml (1 barspoon) crème de violette
15 ml (½ fl oz) VSOP (Very Superior Old Pale) cognac
100 ml (3½ fl oz) champagne
Fresh red rose petals, to garnish

Wet the sugar cube with the Peychaud's Bitters and place it in a coupette. Add the crème de violette and then the cognac. Gently pour in the champagne and garnish with fresh red rose petals floated on top.

FLINT

DIFFICULTY [2]
ABV [1]
FRUITY, HERBAL

Flint was inspired by one of the five elements: Earth. The deep aromas and tastes of cognac and Chartreuse in the Flint are enhanced with Lacto-fermented Melon (page 234). Lacto-fermentation is a method that ferments the fruit with honey and salt, imparting an umami taste not otherwise achieved with regular melon juice. The pomelo and pink pepper tonic water contributes citrus and zest to this exotic blend.

30 ml (1 fl oz) XO cognac
5 ml (1 barspoon) green Chartreuse
20 ml (⅔ fl oz) Lacto-fermented Melon (page 234)
40 ml (1⅓ fl oz) pomelo and pink pepper tonic water

Combine the cognac, Chartreuse, lacto-fermented melon and tonic water in a mixing glass filled with ice and stir until well chilled. Strain into a tumbler filled with ice chunks.

FLOAT LIKE A BUTTERFLY, STING LIKE A BEE

FLOAT LIKE A BUTTERFLY:
DIFFICULTY [3]
ABV [1]
FRUITY, MILKY

STING LIKE A BEE:
DIFFICULTY [2]
ABV [2]
CITRUSY, HONEY

Love is a two-sided affair, one in which both parties share mutual affection and complementary characteristics. This pair of batched champagne cocktails is intended to be served together side by side in celebration of a lovely relationship. Float Like a Butterfly exhibits the complexity of a clarified milk punch made with a flowing stream of distinctive tastes from bourbon, tequila and absinthe, accentuated by vegetal, fruit and herbal notes from the celery, pineapple, fennel seeds, lemon zest, lemon verbena and fresh lemon juice. Sting Like a Bee offers a simpler statement: rich notes of chocolate and dried fruits mingled with fresh lemon juice and touches of floral sweetness from the bee pollen and sugar syrup. Both champagne cocktails complement the attributes of the other, allowing the sipper to appreciate the balance alone or shared with a loved one.

Float Like a Butterfly
45 ml (1½ fl oz) Float Like a Butterfly Milk Punch (page 240)
5 ml (1 barspoon) Sugar Syrup (page 245)
45 ml (1½ fl oz) champagne
2 dashes absinthe
Butterfly sorrel leaf, to garnish

Sting Like a Bee
30 ml (1 fl oz) Bee Pollen-infused Armagnac (page 237)
20 ml (⅔ fl oz) Sugar Syrup (page 245)
15 ml (½ fl oz) fresh lemon juice
30 ml (1 fl oz) champagne
Fresh blue cornflower petals, to garnish

To make Float like a Butterfly: Combine the milk punch, sugar syrup, champagne and absinthe in a mixing glass filled with ice and stir until well chilled. Strain into a flute and garnish with a butterfly sorrel leaf.

To make Sting Like a Bee: Combine the Armagnac, sugar syrup, lemon juice and champagne in a cocktail shaker filled with ice and shake vigorously until the drink is sufficiently chilled. Double strain into a flute decorated with cornflower petals adhered to the side.

FORBIDDEN PASSION

DIFFICULTY ²
ABV NA
FRUITY, GINGERY

According to ancient Iranian Christian teachings, the Garden of Eden's real forbidden fruit was not the apple, it was the pomegranate. Here, we take a childhood classic – the Shirley Temple – and remake it for palates prepared to experience so much more. Our house-made Pomegranate Syrup (page 245) is surprisingly simple to make and worlds better than the commercial versions. Together, this fusion of berries, cranberry and lemon juices and Pomegranate Syrup plays well with the ginger ale, providing a sparkling platform for the fresh berries.

2 fresh raspberries
2 fresh blueberries
2 fresh blackberries
45 ml (1½ fl oz) cranberry juice
20 ml (⅔ fl oz) fresh lemon juice
20 ml (⅔ fl oz) Pomegranate Syrup (page 245)
45 ml (1½ fl oz) ginger ale, for topping
Additional fresh berries, to garnish

Combine the raspberries, blueberries, blackberries, cranberry and lemon juices and syrup in a cocktail shaker filled with ice and shake vigorously until the drink is sufficiently chilled. Double strain into a highball glass over crushed ice and top up with the ginger ale. Garnish with additional fresh berries skewered onto a wooden stick.

FOUNTAIN OF WEALTH

DIFFICULTY [2]
ABV [1]
FRUITY, HERBAL

Who doesn't dream of drinking from a fountain flowing with the wealth of ages and finding themselves richer for the experience? This sophisticated version of a classic Margarita marries reposado tequila (lightly aged tequila) with the richness of fresh pear juice, the dry herbal notes of vermouth and the soft citrus of Lime Sherbet (page 242). The healthy dose of sage tincture adds a magical touch to the aroma and flavour. Did you know that sage leaves are used in magical spells to grant wishes and offer long life to the recipient? Now you know why this cocktail reminds us of the wealth that goes beyond gold. Come drink from this special fountain.

45 ml (1½ fl oz) reposado tequila
30 ml (1 fl oz) fresh pear juice
20 ml (⅔ fl oz) dry vermouth
15 ml (½ fl oz) Lime Sherbet (page 242)
5 ml (1 barspoon) Sage Tincture (page 245)
Dried pear wheels (see page 235) and a grating of nutmeg, to garnish

Place a piece of block ice in a white wine glass. Combine the tequila, pear juice, vermouth, sherbet and tincture in a cocktail shaker filled with ice and shake vigorously until the drink is sufficiently chilled. Double strain into the glass and garnish with dried pear wheels skewered onto a wooden stick and a grating of nutmeg.

GARIBALDINO

DIFFICULTY [2]
ABV [1]
CITRUSY, FRUITY

Giuseppe Maria Garibaldi was a nineteenth-century Italian who gained notoriety for his contribution to the unification of the Italian states. He was also instrumental in the creation of the Kingdom of Italy, along with the new nation's first king, Victor Emmanuel II, and the revolutionary movement's champion, Giuseppe Mazzini. A salute to this 'father of the fatherland', the Garibaldino unites a bright citrus palate with the floral notes of Italicus Rosolio di Bergamotto, an Italian liqueur produced from rose petals and bergamot oranges. The sparkle from the white grape and apricot soda marries this palette of Italian flavours gathered from diverse regions of this bountiful country into a light, refreshing experience.
In case you are unfamiliar with Savoia American Rosso Amaro Dolce, it is a bittersweet aperitif with notes of gentian and bitter orange.

30 ml (1 fl oz) London dry gin
30 ml (1 fl oz) Italicus Rosolio di Bergamotto
30 ml (1 fl oz) Savoia Americano Rosso Amaro Dolce
20 ml (⅔ fl oz) Clementine and Tonka Bean Shrub (page 243)
60 ml (2 fl oz) white grape and apricot soda
Red Lime Disc Water Cake (page 236), to garnish

Combine the gin, Italicus Rosolio di Bergamotto, Savoia, shrub and soda in a mixing glass filled with ice and stir until well chilled. Strain into a rocks glass with a piece of block ice and garnish with a water cake.

GENTLEMAN SPRITZ

DIFFICULTY [2]
ABV [2]
BITTER, FRUITY

This fruit-driven nod to a classic Italian aperitif cocktail – the Spritz – is a logical evolution. Twentieth-century journalist Charles H. Baker documented the best drinks served around the world in his 1939 book *The Gentleman's Companion: Being an Exotic Drinking Book or, Around the World with Jigger, Beaker and Flask*. At the Repulse Bay Hotel in Hong Kong, he encountered a magnificent version of the Spritz. Thankfully, he documented it, leaving us the inspiration for this drink.

25 ml (¾ fl oz) Calvados
25 ml (¾ fl oz) Rhubarb and Red Fruits Cordial (page 233)
10 ml (⅓ fl oz) Galliano l'Aperitivo
60 ml (2 fl oz) champagne
Fresh apple blossom (begonia) edible flowers, to garnish

Combine the Calvados, Galliano l'Aperitivo and champagne in a mixing glass filled with ice and stir until well chilled. Strain into a red wine glass filled with a big ice chunk and garnish with fresh apple blossom (begonia) edible flowers.

GIVE IT THE GREEN LIGHT

DIFFICULTY [3]
ABV [1]
FRUITY, SAVOURY

'Give it the green light' is a phrase that indicates a project has been given the go-ahead. And this drink commemorates the day we got the green light to open the Connaught Bar in its new vision. The green light came at the end of June 2008, when we set out to build our dream bar, bar team and drinks menu, and to attract our dream guests. Our dreams came true. Just like the Connaught Bar itself, there is far more to this drink than meets the eye. It is hard to define the sum of these elements. There are hints of Martini character, hints of Bloody Mary flavour and an herbaceous tone completed by the sharpness of the sorrel leaves. More than a twist on cocktail history, this drink was inspired by the art of mixology and the hotel management who celebrate the hotel's bar culture as an oasis of culinary art.

50 ml (1¾ fl oz) Passion Berry and Grapeseed Oil-washed Vodka
(page 234)
20 ml (⅔ fl oz) Tomato skin-infused Japanese Gin (page 237)
3 dashes Electric Bitters
20 ml (⅔ fl oz) Osmanthus and Timur Pepper Syrup (page 245)
Fresh green sorrel leaves, to garnish

Combine the vodka, gin, bitters, syrup and vodka in a mixing glass filled with ice and stir until well chilled. Strain into a coupette with a piece of block ice and garnish with fresh green sorrel leaves set on top of the ice.

GLOOM DAISY

DIFFICULTY [2]
ABV [1]
SMOKY, FRUITY

Drinks that promised to raise your spirits were popular during the 1930s, '40s and beyond. In his 1948 book *The Fine Art of Mixing Drinks*, David A. Embury challenged his readers to compare the Gloom Lifter with the Gloom Chaser and the Gloom Raiser. This twist on Embury's Gloom Lifter – basically a classic cocktail called an egg sour made with Irish whiskey – adds some delightful fruit touches to a classic combination. The result is a crisp, dry, smoky drink with elegant raspberry and pomegranate notes that is light and deceptively strong.

15 ml (½ fl oz) raspberry purée
15 ml (½ fl oz) egg white
20 ml (⅔ fl oz) fresh lemon juice
20 ml (⅔ fl oz) Pomegranate Syrup (page 245)
50 ml (1¾ fl oz) 12-year-old peated Scotch whisky
Fresh raspberry, to garnish

Whizz the purée, egg white, lemon juice, syrup and whisky with a hand-held blender. Or you can dry shake the ingredients in a cocktail shaker without ice, then hard shake the mixture with ice cubes. Strain into a white wine glass and garnish with a fresh raspberry.

GOOD FELLAS

DIFFICULTY ³
ABV ¹
BALSAMIC, SMOKY

'As far as I can remember I always wanted to be a gangster' is a quote from the 1990 film *Goodfellas* that inspired Giorgio in 2015 to create a modern twist on the Fanciulli – a sweet Manhattan found in Albert Stevens Crockett's 1934 book *The Old Waldorf-Astoria Bar Book*. The drink was served as a frappé or straight up. While the original recipe added a fernet-style amaro – a popular bitter aromatic Italian spirit served as a digestif – to the traditional blend of whiskey and vermouth, Giorgio's version highlights techniques and tastes that are essential to the modern mixological repertoire. Fresh cardamom leaves are infused into the bourbon and the pungent character of black cardamom is highlighted in our house-made syrup. The recent revival of Abbott's Bitters offers the drink hints of tonka bean (see page 256), peppermint, sweet cinnamon and warm spices. (But you can opt to use Angostura Bitters, if you prefer.) The deep notes of fig, molasses and cherry from the balsamic vinegar provide a finishing touch of mellow tartness. The hint of elicriso essence, extracted from *Helichrysum orientale* flowers, tops the bill with a floral note. If you can't get this essence, sage and wormwood tincture will work just as well. As befits its name, the Good Fellas is a cheeky, lively take on a memorable classic cocktail.

2 dashes Abbott's Bitters
5 ml (1 barspoon) balsamic vinegar
10 ml (⅓ fl oz) Black Cardamom Seed Syrup (page 244)
25 ml (¾ fl oz) Italian red vermouth
50 ml (1¾ fl oz) Fresh Cardamom Leaf-infused Bourbon (page 237)
Spray of elicriso essence
Bourbon cherry, to garnish

Place a piece of block ice in a red wine glass. Vigorously shake the bitters, vinegar, syrup, vermouth, bourbon and ice cubes in a cocktail shaker. Strain into the glass and spray the elicriso essence over the top, then suspend a bourbon cherry over the edge of the glass (we suspend it from a little belt that fastens around the glass).

HIDDEN PARK

DIFFICULTY [2]
ABV [1]
HERBAL, WINEY

Shinrin yoku, the Japanese concept of 'forest bathing', is a simple method of finding tranquillity in natural spaces. Our Hidden Park conceals its special notes of Szechuan peppercorns in a breath of basil that heightens the gin's cucumber and rose character. The floral character of the Riesling wine and the soft citrus notes of pink grapefruit open new horizons in your understanding of the complexity of the new gins and the cocktails that are made with them. The *wakamomo*, a pickled young peach from Japan, adds a finishing touch of slightly sweet and sour character to the ensemble.

30 ml (1 fl oz) cucumber and rose gin
20 ml (⅔ fl oz) Riesling wine
25 ml (¾ fl oz) Clarified Grapefruit Juice (page 232)
20 ml (⅔ fl oz) Basil and Szechuan Pepper Syrup (page 244)
Wakamomo, to garnish

Combine the gin, wine, grapefruit juice and syrup in a mixing glass filled with ice and stir until well chilled. Strain into a flute and garnish with a wakamomo speared onto the end of a cocktail sword.

IMPERIAL COSSACK CRUSTA

DIFFICULTY [1]
ABV [1]
SOUR, SPICY

Only journalist-cum-globetrotter Charles H. Baker could unearth a champagne concoction at the home of a friend who lived in the French Concession of Shanghai, which he imported from Russia when the aristocracy took flight eastward in advance of revolutionary forces. Baker documented this rare find in his 1939 drinks travelogue *The Gentleman's Companion*. The vision of a drink that he recounted conjures up images of beautifully regal Russian princesses with every sip and inspired this modern twist. It has a deep, complex character of genever, absinthe and drops of Abbott's Bitters, accented with a fresh palate of elderflower liqueur and lemon juice. This updated version of a refreshingly frosty, luxurious crusta bears regal notes not just from its sweet, golden rim but from the rich aromas and tastes it grants with every sip.

Neutral spirit, for spraying the glass
Edible gold powder and granulated sugar, for dusting the glass
50 ml (1¾ fl oz) genever
5 ml (1 barspoon) absinthe
5 ml (1 barspoon) elderflower liqueur
20 ml (⅔ fl oz) fresh lemon juice
10 ml (⅓ fl oz) Sugar Syrup (page 245)
Drops of Abbott's Bitters
50 ml (1¾ fl oz) champagne

Spray one side of a red wine glass with a neutral spirit and dust the same side of the glass with edible gold powder and granulated sugar with the help of a powder decorating shaker. Combine the genever, absinthe, liqueur, lemon juice, sugar syrup and bitters in a cocktail shaker filled with ice. Strain into the prepared glass and top with the champagne.

THE INNOCENT BENTLEY COCKTAIL

DIFFICULTY ²
ABV NA
TANGY, FRUITY

This cocktail was created at the request of the Bentley motor company in 2016 to serve as a non-alcoholic version of The Bentley Cocktail (page 48). The drink was made to be prepared in advance and served in the vehicle's small bar. Flavours are some of our most enduring memories, some reaching back to childhood. We never stop making these reminiscences. Here, combining classic flavour memories in a new structure, we sought to create a pleasant new recollection. Refreshing and indulgent, the combination of our house-made Rhubarb and Red Fruits Cordial (page 233) with the highest quality of organic cloudy apple juice and pink grapefruit soda creates a balance of tastes unlike any other.

60 ml (2 fl oz) organic cloudy apple juice
30 ml (1 fl oz) Rhubarb and Red Fruits Cordial (page 233)
90 ml (3 fl oz) pink grapefruit soda
Fresh apple blossom (begonia) edible flowers, to garnish

Combine the apple juice and cordial in a cocktail shaker filled with ice and shake vigorously until the drink is sufficiently chilled. Strain into a highball glass over ice, top with the pink grapefruit soda and garnish with fresh apple blossom (begonia) edible flowers.

ITALIAN JOB

DIFFICULTY [1]
ABV [1]
FRUITY, BITTER

This drink appeared on our first menu as a seasonal option. Fruity with a light, dry finish, the Italian Job can be customized to suit your mood or to express a special moment. Although the recipe appears to be a passion fruit Martini with an Italian touch of the most famous bitter aperitif – Campari – you can make it your own by trying it with a different fruit purée such as mango or papaya. The possibilities are endless.

50 ml (1¾ fl oz) vodka
15 ml (½ fl oz) Sugar Syrup (page 245)
20 ml (⅔ fl oz) fresh lime juice
30 ml (1 fl oz) passion fruit purée
30 ml (1 fl oz) pineapple juice
10 ml (⅓ fl oz) Campari
½ passion fruit, pulp scooped out
½ passion fruit, to garnish

Combine the vodka, sugar syrup, lime juice, purée, pineapple juice, Campari and passion fruit pulp in a cocktail shaker filled with ice and shake vigorously until the drink is sufficiently chilled. Double strain into a chilled cocktail glass, then float the passion fruit on top.

THE JENKINS

DIFFICULTY ³
ABV ²
DRY, FLORAL

Founded in 1901, John Jenkins designs and manufactures bespoke glassware, including the Connaught Bar's custom-designed house glassware. This cocktail is dedicated to the company's master craftspeople. Just like the glassmaker's elegant designs, this creation delivers unique touches that you would not expect. Clear and crisp, The Jenkins delivers a herbal punch from the Everleaf Forest non-alcoholic aperitif and expresses a hint of almonds from the apricot kernels (pits) in the pisco infusion.

25 ml (¾ fl oz) Passion Fruit Seed-infused Vodka (page 239)
25 ml (¾ fl oz) Apricot Kernel-infused Pisco (page 238)
15 ml (½ fl oz) elderflower liqueur
10 ml (⅓ fl oz) Everleaf Forest
60 ml (2 fl oz) champagne
Clear Isomalt Spikes (page 236)

Combine the vodka, pisco, liqueur, Everleaf Forest and champagne in a mixing glass filled with ice and stir until well chilled. Strain into a white wine glass filled with ice. Garnish with several clear isomalt spikes, which resemble shards of glass.

JUNO

DIFFICULTY [2]
ABV [1]
MINTY, CHOCOLATY

Juno was the Roman goddess of love and marriage. Her name has long been associated with the renewal – or rejuvenation – of the new moon. This gin creation evokes the quarter moon that shines on each Connaught Bar mirrored table. It also invites you to reflect on the half-moon shaped piece of white chocolate that graces this refreshingly light cocktail. The floral fresh notes of the cucumber and rose gin and jasmine tea are complemented by the herbaceous notes from the Acqua Bianca liqueur, a complex blend of lemon verbena, bergamot, peppermint, rose and a hint of ambergris. The mint soda and Cocoa Husk Cream (page 239) marry these diverse flavours into a luscious veil of smoothness.

45 ml (1½ fl oz) cucumber and rose gin
30 ml (1 fl oz) Cocoa Husk Cream (page 239)
30 ml (1 fl oz) brewed jasmine tea
10 ml (⅓ fl oz) Acqua Bianca liqueur
10 ml (⅓ fl oz) fresh lemon juice
30 ml (1 fl oz) mint soda
Half-moon-shaped piece of white chocolate, to garnish

Combine the gin, cocoa husk cream, jasmine tea, liqueur, lemon juice and soda in a mixing glass filled with ice and stir until well chilled. Strain into a Kyoto glass filled with ice and garnish with a half-moon-shaped piece of white chocolate.

KNICKERBOCKER PUNCH

DIFFICULTY ³
ABV ¹
SOUR, HERBAL

Charles H. Baker, the renowned American journalist and cocktail aficionado, devoted his travels and time to documenting some of the finest sips he discovered as he globetrotted throughout the first half of the twentieth century. He waxed nostalgic with a 'memory of the good days of 1915' when he recalled the signature drink at New York's Hotel Knickerbocker – the training ground for such famed barmen as Eddie Woelke, who went on to head Havana's Sevilla-Biltmore bar, and Harry Craddock, who presided over London's American Bar at the Savoy during the 1920s and '30s. This twist on the hotel's The Knickerbocker 'Punch' is reminiscent of those bygone days of sipping in one of the world's great hotel bars. A delicate, dry yet creamy sip thanks to the inclusion of egg white, the aromas and tastes of Lime Sherbet (page 242) and fragrant lemon verbena accentuate the Makrut Lime Leaf-infused Genever (page 237) with its complex rye and barley notes. The champagne adds characteristic sparkle while the raspberry brings hits of fruitiness to this modern, frothy interpretation. It brings a smile to the face of anyone who encounters it.

Neutral spirit, for spraying the glass
Raspberry Sugar (page 244), for dusting the glass
50 ml (1¾ fl oz) Makrut Lime Leaf-infused Genever (page 237)
30 ml (1 fl oz) Lime Sherbet (page 242)
15 ml (½ fl oz) egg white or pasteurized egg white
5 ml (1 barspoon) Lemon Verbena Sugar (page 243)
50 ml (1¾ fl oz) champagne
Spray of Angostura Bitters, to garnish

Spray one side of a coupette with a neutral spirit and dust the same side of the glass with raspberry sugar with the help of a powder decorating shaker. Whizz the genever, sherbet, egg white and sugar with a hand-held blender in a shaker tin. Alternatively, you can hard shake the ingredients in a cocktail shaker without ice, then add the ice and shake vigorously so the mixture becomes frothy. Strain into the prepared coupette.
Top with champagne and garnish with a spray of Angostura Bitters.

LA LAMBADA

DIFFICULTY [1]
ABV NA
MILKY, CITRUSY

A star was born at the Caribe Hilton in San Juan, Puerto Rico, in the summer of 1954, when pineapple juice met coconut cream. The combination is so delicious that the rum seems almost an afterthought, as this rich and indulgent non-alcoholic drink demonstrates. The fresh lemongrass, lime juice and bitter lemon soda add a completely new dimension. The result is irresistible and was featured on our first menu.

30 ml (1 fl oz) fresh pineapple juice
30 ml (1 fl oz) coconut cream
15 ml (½ fl oz) fresh lime juice
3 fresh lemongrass straws, one cut in half
100 ml (3½ fl oz) bitter lemon soda
Mint sprig, to garnish

Muddle the pineapple juice, coconut cream, lime juice and the halved lemongrass straw in a cocktail shaker filled with ice, then shake vigorously until the drink is sufficiently chilled. Double strain into a highball glass over crushed ice. Top up with the bitter lemon soda and garnish with the remaining lemongrass straws and a mint sprig.

LATINA DAISY

DIFFICULTY [1]
ABV [2]
SOUR, CHOCOLATY

You may have experienced and loved many modern classics that fall under the drink category known as the Daisy – a sour cocktail sweetened with a liqueur or flavoured syrup. The Cosmopolitan, the Daiquirí and the Margarita (Spanish for 'daisy') are all Daisies. I crafted this Latina Daisy in 2008, to embrace the sensual experiences of Latin and Cuban culture – the colours, aromas, flavours and lifestyle. A classically crisp, fresh sour cocktail, it pairs dark chocolate liqueur with the crisp, fresh, lightly fruity character of white Cuban rum plus its distinctive notes of marzipan, citrus and allspice. This experience is heightened by the anise notes from the fennel seeds as well as the anise and vanilla dominant liqueur. Every sip of the Latina Daisy imparts a distinctive complexity, sophistication and richness to the palate. It can be served as an aperitif, digestif or simply as a delightful afternoon refreshment with a piece of rich, dark chocolate. My Latina Daisy was the winning creation at the 2009 Bacardí Legacy bartending competition.

100% organic cocoa powder, for decorating the rim of the glass
1 lime half, for moistening the rim of the glass
10 ml (⅓ fl oz) Galliano l'Autentico
25 ml (¾ fl oz) fresh lime juice
1–2 barspoons white caster (superfine) sugar
2 barspoons fennel seeds
50 ml (1¾ fl oz) white Cuban rum
20 ml (⅔ fl oz) dark crème de cacao

Spread some cocoa powder out on a plate. Prepare a coupette by moistening the rim with a lime half at a 45-degree angle and then dip the rim of the glass in the cocoa powder until coated. Pour the Galliano l'Autentico into the coupette to give the drink a silky texture and clear appearance. Combine the lime juice, sugar and fennel seeds in a cocktail shaker and lightly muddle to dissolve the sugar and express the character of the fennel seeds. By mixing the sugar and lime juice in this way, you get a crisper texture and flavour. Add the rum and crème de cacao and some ice cubes to the shaker, then shake and double strain into the prepared coupette.

LEMON NOIR

DIFFICULTY [1]
ABV [2]
LEMONY, SMOKY

A style of film-making that exploits stark lighting effects as it portrays intricate and often surprising plot twists, cinema noir inspired the name for this twist on a French 75, popularized in the 1920s by famed barman Harry MacElhone at the New York Bar in Paris. This dark version of the French 75 conceals a hidden secret: the Swiss lemon crème palate camouflaged in this charcoal black, effervescent concoction. Featuring London dry gin, yuzu and our house-made Baked Lemon Syrup (page 244), this very noir refreshment reveals its surprise ending in the first sip.

Edible silver paint, to decorate the glass
25 ml (⅔ fl oz) London dry gin
15 ml (½ fl oz) Yuzu Juice (page 235)
15 ml (½ fl oz) Baked Lemon Syrup (page 244)
60 ml (2 fl oz) champagne

Paint a flute with a stripe of edible silver paint and set aside. Combine the gin, yuzu juice and syrup in a cocktail shaker filled with ice and shake vigorously until the drink is sufficiently chilled. Double strain into a flute and gently add the champagne.

MADAME D

DIFFICULTY ³
ABV ¹
Milky, nutty

Dedicated to Hélène Darroze, head chef at the restaurant Hélène Darroze at the Connaught, this drink was inspired by flavours she encountered as a child growing up in the Armagnac region of France. Forget what your senses tell you, the Madame D conjures up something truly out of the ordinary with delicate hints of spice. The tequila takes on a remarkable rich softness after spending a night with the peanut and almond butters. The Clarified Vanilla Milk (page 232) adds creaminess without compromising clarity. Combined with the deep aromas of barrel-aged Armagnac and the toasty effervescence of champagne, this libation transports you into new dimensions in the cocktail universe.

15 ml (½ fl oz) barrel-aged Armagnac
15 ml (½ fl oz) Almond and Peanut Butters-washed Reposado Tequila (page 233)
45 ml (1½ fl oz) Clarified Vanilla Milk (page 232)
30 ml (1 fl oz) champagne
Piece of dark chocolate, to garnish

Pour the Armagnac, tequila, milk and champagne into a cocktail shaker filled with ice and throw the liquid (see page 17) between the two shakers. Strain into a coupette over a piece of block ice and garnish with a piece of dark chocolate set on top of the ice.

MADAME PICKFORD

DIFFICULTY [3]
ABV [1]
FRUITY, CHOCOLATY

He may have never written a cocktail book, but Basil Woon immortalized the Mary Pickford cocktail in his 1928 travelogue *When It's Cocktail Time in Cuba*, when he noted that Liverpudlian bartender Fred Kaufman was 'the inventor of many cocktails in which pineapple juice is the chief ingredient'. Kaufman's most enduring creation – a cocktail made with rum, pineapple juice and grenadine – was crafted for silent-screen star Mary Pickford when she stayed at Havana's Hotel Nacional. The drink embodies simplicity. We decided to make this enduring cocktail more sophisticated by infusing aged whisky with roasted pineapple and enhancing it with the rich, luscious flavours of cocoa, an herbaceous amaro and maraschino liqueur. The mint leaves add a touch of freshness to a cocktail bouquet that deserves deference and respect.

40 ml (1⅓ fl oz) Roasted Pineapple-infused Aged Blended Scotch (page 238)
10 ml (⅓ fl oz) pomegranate molasses
20 ml (⅔ fl oz) Cocoa Bean-infused Amaro Lucano (page 236)
5 ml (1 barspoon) maraschino liqueur
6 mint leaves
1 cocktail cherry and 2 white chocolate triangles, to garnish

Swizzle the whisky, pomegranate molasses, amaro, liqueur and mint leaves in a silver julep cup with a little crushed ice. When blended, add more crushed ice to fill. Garnish with a cocktail cherry and white chocolate triangles.

MAGNETUM

DIFFICULTY ³
ABV ²
RICH, FRUITY

They say opposites attract. In the Magnetum, art and science collide to create a visually striking drink. The clear liquid in the bottom represents the outside of the Connaught Bar and the dark brown liquid layered on top represents the venue's interior. Using a bespoke ice lift that reduces dilution while it elevates the piece of block ice in the drink, the liquids are married together, blending tradition and innovation, form and flavour into a single statement. The patterned base of the ice lift offers an additional visual element to savour as you sip. The bottom layer is a clarified whisky milk punch featuring fresh pineapple and fino sherry with hints of fennel and lemon verbena. The top layer is single malt whisky and a Pedro Ximénez sherry. When the two layers merge as one, they create a rich, fruity sip with warm undertones of walnuts, wood smoke and crème brûlée. This is a deep sip to be shared over a long conversation, a dish of nuts, dried fruits and a piece of Manchego or other sheep's milk cheese. We created the bespoke ice lift tool to lift a piece of block ice inside an old fashioned glass, but a barspoon can be used to blend the liquids together.

75 ml (2½ fl oz) Magnetum Milk Punch (page 240)
30 ml (1 fl oz) Magnetum Sherry-whisky Mix (page 241)

Place a piece of block ice in a rocks glass, resting on a bespoke ice lift. Carefully pour the milk punch into the prepared glass. Layer the sherry-whisky mix into the glass. Lift the block of ice up to incorporate the two liquids, then serve.

MANILA HOTEL MINT JULEP

DIFFICULTY [2]
ABV [2]
FRUITY, MINTY

Journalist-cum-globetrotter Charles H. Baker's love of Mint Juleps fills a staggering eight pages in his 1939 drinks travelogue *The Gentleman's Companion*. He began by citing the concoction's ancient Persian origins before extolling the joys of Kentucky Mint Juleps. Baker then continued his homage by presenting eight formulas he encountered in the Philippines, Cuba, Kentucky, Georgia, Tennessee and Maryland. It was bartender Monk Antrim's Manila Hotel Mint Julep No. 1 that captured our attention, combining bourbon and rum with pineapple as a tropical touch. This twist on Baker's discovery introduces the lightly spiced and bittersweet notes of Amaro Braulio, an Italian amaro with deep flavours of clove, dried fruits, cola, liquorice and bitter bark, in addition to the marriage of cognac and rum from the Dominican Republic. The complexity of this refresher is enhanced, like its predecessor, with pineapple notes as well as a traditional signature of fresh mint leaves.

20 ml (⅔ fl oz) Amaro Braulio
30 ml (1 fl oz) Dominican Republic-style rum
20 ml (⅔ fl oz) cognac
25 ml (¾ fl oz) Pineapple and Rosemary Shrub (page 243)
6 fresh mint leaves
Rosemary sprig and a dried pineapple slice (see page 235), to garnish

Swizzle the amaro, rum, cognac, shrub and mint leaves in a silver julep cup with a little crushed ice. When blended, top with more crushed ice and garnish with a rosemary sprig and a dried pineapple slice.

MAYFAIR LADY

DIFFICULTY [3]
ABV [1]
FLORAL, SPICY

Professor Henry Higgins: By George, she's got it! By George, she's got it!
Now, once again where does it rain?
Eliza Doolittle: [sings] On the plain! On the plain!
Professor Henry Higgins: And where's that soggy plain?
Eliza Doolittle: [sings] In Spain! In Spain!

My Fair Lady (1964)

A twist on the Mayfair Cocktail, which Robert Vermeire invented and featured in his 1922 book *Cocktails: How to Mix Them*, our Mayfair Lady was inspired by a gregarious waitress who previously worked in the Connaught Bar. A tequila-based cocktail, it embodies the spice-forward profile of the original, which included dashes of both apricot and clove syrups, by infusing the spices into Sancerre wine and accentuating the aroma with elderflower liqueur. With her new-found flavour language, our Mayfair Lady ventures out into new and far more refined territory.

25 ml (¾ fl oz) Walnut Oil-washed Reposado Tequila (page 234)
30 ml (1 fl oz) Spice-infused Sancerre Wine (page 239)
10 ml (⅓ fl oz) elderflower liqueur
Fresh blue cornflower, to garnish

Combine the tequila, wine and liqueur in a mixing glass filled with ice and stir until well chilled. Strain into a white wine glass over a chunk of ice and garnish with a fresh blue cornflower set on top of the ice.

MEDITERRANEAN SODA

DIFFICULTY [2]
ABV [1]
CITRUSY, TANGY

This clean, crisp thirst quencher harkens back to fresh, fragrant breezes and lazy, sunny days on the Mediterranean. This refreshing highball features the slightly piney flavour and aroma of mastiha, a Greek liqueur made from the resin of the mastic tree, a small evergreen that is native to the Mediterranean. Scents of bergamot, basil and mastiha waft in the air and on the palate. A delicate bite of aromatic spice from the angel hair chilli – dried and shredded Chinese long chillies that impart a citrusy flavour – brightens the experience without adding too much heat.

50 ml (1¾ fl oz) vodka
30 ml (1 fl oz) Bergamot and Basil Sherbet (page 242)
15 ml (½ fl oz) mastiha
100 ml (3½ fl oz) pink grapefruit soda
Small cluster of angel hair chilli, to garnish

Combine the vodka, sherbet, mastiha and soda in a mixing glass filled with ice and stir until well chilled. Strain into a highball glass filled with ice and garnish with a small cluster of angel hair chilli.

MEMENTO

DIFFICULTY ³
ABV ³
HERBAL, MINERAL

The Memento is an updated version of a Connaught Bar classic, Set in Stone (page 194). It is also a modernized twist on a cocktail classic, the Martinez. While the latter blends gin, sweet vermouth and maraschino liqueur with a dash of bitters, our version marries cucumber and rose gin with genever to add more complexity to the foundation botanical mixture. In a similar vein, the warmth of sherry is paired with dry vermouth to establish a richer tone than its ancestor. In the same way we contributed stone to the Set in Stone presentation, we sous-vide the Memento Mix (page 241) with a piece of white marble and heat it to impart a touch of chalk and dry sweet to the finished drink. The piece of stone paper (a paper made from discarded stone), spray of elicriso essence, extracted from *Helichrysum orientale* flowers, and a *wakamomo* – pickled young peach from Japan – add the finishing touches of slightly herbal, sweet and sour pickle character to the presentation.

Piece of stone paper
90 ml (3 fl oz) Memento Mix (page 241)
Spray of elicriso essence
Wakamomo, to garnish

Place a piece of stone paper under a big chunk of ice into a white wine glass. Add the Memento mix to a cocktail shaker filled with ice and shake vigorously until the drink is sufficiently chilled. Double strain into the prepared glass, spray with the essence and garnish with a wakamomo skewered onto a cocktail pick.

MY FAIR

DIFFICULTY [2]
ABV [1]
SOUR, SPICY

The Mayfair Cocktail, named after one of London's most aristocratic neighbourhoods, made its way around Europe at the height of Prohibition in the United States. Robert Vermiere, in his 1922 book *Cocktails: How to Mix Them*, claims he created the recipe while working at the Embassy Club in London in 1921. Harry Cradddock added a touch of spice to his version, which appeared in his 1930 compilation *The Savoy Cocktail Book*. Our My Fair tips a glass not only to this cocktail classic but also to the district in which the Connaught resides. We've added a sparkle to our presentation with a touch of champagne, which accentuates the aromas and flavours of our house-made Spiced Calamansi Sherbet (page 242) and Apricot Velvet (page 235) that make My Fair a special tribute of our own.

35 ml (1¼ fl oz) gin
30 ml (1 fl oz) Spicy Calamansi Sherbet (page 242)
30 ml (1 fl oz) Cocchi Americano
2 dashes Abbott's Bitters
50 ml (1¾ fl oz) champagne
50 ml (1¾ fl oz) Apricot Velvet (page 235)
Piece of silver leaf, to garnish

Combine the gin, sherbet, Cocchi Americano and bitters in a cocktail shaker filled with ice and shake vigorously until the drink is sufficiently chilled. Double strain into a Kyoto glass. Top up with the champagne and slightly stir, then top with the apricot velvet and garnish with a piece of silver leaf.

MYSTERIOUS WOODLANDS

DIFFICULTY ³
ABV ²
EARTHY, WOODY

No matter where you wander, there is a certain mystique to a walk in the woods. It's no wonder forests and woodlands are ideal locations for those who seek tranquility, and even a hint of mystery. The intensity of the sweet earthy notes of the Beetroot and Blackberry Cordial (page 233) in our Mysterious Woodlands is calmed by the introduction of cocoa and citrus notes. The aroma of the spinach and lemon thyme powder touches your senses with a profusion of matcha-like notes that make you feel like you are walking in the woods.

Neutral spirit, for spraying the glass
Dried spinach and lemon thyme powder, for dusting the glass
50 ml (1¾ fl oz) Cocoa Bean-infused Vodka (page 238)
10 ml (⅓ fl oz) fresh lime juice
20 ml (⅔ fl oz) Beetroot and Blackberry Cordial (page 233)
2 dashes orange-mandarin bitters or orange bitters

Spray one side of a white wine glass with a neutral spirit and dust the same side of the glass with dried spinach and lemon powder with the help of a powder decorating shaker. Add a piece of block ice to the glass. Combine the vodka, lime juice, cordial and bitters in a cocktail shaker filled with ice and shake vigorously until the drink is sufficiently chilled. Double strain into the prepared glass.

MYSTERY OF SIMPLICITY

DIFFICULTY [3]
ABV [2]
FRUITY, ALMONDY

Look, then look again. Classic ingredients are given an unexpected twist and the ordinary becomes extraordinary in this beguiling blend of apple and oak floating in a sea of deep, rich rum. Our Mystery of Simplicity may have a foundation in aged rums, but it is not all wood and heavy tastes. The Fermented Green Apple (page 234) and Almond Sherbet (page 242) contribute fruit and spice to the equation. The sparkling oakwood tonic water and sherry add a touch of increased complexity that begs for you to come back for more.

25 ml (¾ fl oz) Afro-Caribbean rum
20 ml (⅔ fl oz) banana rum
30 ml (1 fl oz) oloroso sherry
15 ml (½ fl oz) Fermented Green Apple (page 234)
10 ml (⅓ fl oz) Almond Sherbet (page 242)
30 ml (1 fl oz) oakwood tonic water
Piece of fresh banana leaf, to garnish

Combine the rums, sherry, fermented green apple, sherbet and tonic water in a mixing glass filled with ice and stir until well chilled. Strain into a red wine glass with a piece of block ice and garnish with a piece of fresh banana leaf.

NEGRONI 10–100

DIFFICULTY ³
ABV ²
BITTER, DRY

Presented in 2019 for the one-hundredth anniversary of the Negroni, with Connaught Gin, the Negroni 10–100 was actually born in 2018 to celebrate the tenth anniversary of the Connaught Bar. The drink was originally layered in the glass and mixed by the guest. Each element in the drink has a big personality. This twist on the Negroni uses rare botanicals, a new blend of a floral and honey-laced vermouth di Torino – Martini Riserva Speciale Ambrato – and rediscovered vintage flavours. Considered a simple drink throughout the first century of its life, the Negroni's cardinal structure, balancing strength, bitter, sweet and spice, is a perfect springboard for flavour exploration. After extensive experimentation we landed on this lush and luxurious interpretation of Italy's most iconic aperitif. The hint of Bordeaux wine adds a new dimension.

15 ml (½ fl oz) Evanish Bordeaux Wine (page 245)
10 ml (⅓ fl oz) Galliano l'Aperitivo
30 ml (1 fl oz) gin
20 ml (⅔ fl oz) Martini Riserva Speciale Ambrato
Spray of orange leaf food-grade essential oil, to garnish

Layer the wine and Galliano l'Aperitivo, then the gin and Ambrato in a red wine glass over a ball of ice or ice sphere and garnish with a spray of orange leaf essential oil.

THE NEW ABBEY

DIFFICULTY ²
ABV ²
CHOCOLATY, ORANGEY

Nearly a century after its debut in Harry Craddock's 1930 *The Savoy Cocktail Book*, the Abbey Cocktail is still a tried-and-true classic mix of gin, Lillet, orange juice and Angostura Bitters. It also proves to be an ideal stepping stone for the creation of a new drink. Thus, we gave it the name The New Abbey in tribute to its inspiration. We have no doubt Harry Craddock would have loved the broad spectrum of flavours and techniques available to modern bartenders. While fat-washing (see page 66) exploded onto the bar scene in the early 2000s, it has never delivered better taste than with cocoa butter and coconut oil. And green mandarin essence? It has become as indispensable as Angostura Bitters. These days, we can evoke any season through essences and bitters, as well as capturing flavours through fat-washing our spirits.

50 ml (1¾ fl oz) Cocoa Butter-washed Vodka (page 234)
20 ml (⅔ fl oz) fresh orange juice
10 ml (⅓ fl oz) Sugar Syrup (page 245)
5 dashes coriander bitters
Spray of green mandarin essence
Small white chocolate disc and a large white chocolate disc, to garnish

Combine the vodka, orange juice, sugar syrup and bitters in a cocktail shaker filled with ice and shake vigorously until the drink is sufficiently chilled. Double strain into a coupette, spray the top with green mandarin essence and garnish with the discs of white chocolate.

NUMBER 11

DIFFICULTY ²
ABV ³
DRY, AROMATIC

Number 11 was created in 2019 to celebrate the Connaught Bar's eleventh anniversary. A tribute and an evolution of The Connaught Martini (page 24), our bar's signature offering, it was also inspired by another cocktail classic, The Vesper. While the Number 11 only contains four ingredients, there are two elements that make this version a special occasion, a visual celebration. First, the cocktail glass is hand painted with splashes of edible art paint in a style reminiscent of the famed twentieth-century Abstract Expressionist painter Jackson Pollock. The four colours we use represent the drink's four main ingredients: gin, vodka, vermouth and bitters. (The drink also adopts Pollock's technique for naming his works by number.) Second, the drink is aerated in the same way Spanish cider is served, using an *escanciador*, a battery-operated Spanish cider-pouring device that injects air into the drink by just pouring the liquid from a great height. (The same aeration can be accomplished by throwing the drink, see page 17, just like they do in Barcelona.) To craft this new classic, gin, vodka and our house-made Amalfi Lemon Peel-infused Vermouth (page 238) are batched in a bottle and stored in the freezer. The quantities below are for an individual Number 11, but we recommend making ten portions – 450 ml (15 fl oz) gin, 300 ml (10 fl oz) vodka and 150 ml (5 fl oz) vermouth – so you have more than one serving in the bottle. To serve, the frozen bottle is attached to the escanciador and dispensed into the hand-painted cocktail glass. A delicate rose-like fragrance is imparted to the presentation when a few dashes of bitters distilled from the same five aromatic bitters that are also offered with The Connaught Martini (ginseng-bergamot, lavender, tonka bean, coriander and cardamom) are dropped on the top. The resulting delicate, aromatic notes of citrus and spice are guaranteed to excite to the senses.

Edible paints, to decorate the glass
45 ml (1½ fl oz) gin
30 ml (1 fl oz) vodka
15 ml (½ fl oz) Amalfi Lemon Peel-infused Vermouth (page 238)
1–2 dashes five bitters distillate (or you can substitute orange flower water)

Freely splash dots of edible paint in at least four colours onto a coupette and leave to dry. Pour the gin, vodka and vermouth into a sterilized bottle. Freeze the bottle until ready to serve. Attach the frozen bottle to an *escanciador*. Turn it on and dispense the drink into the decorated cocktail glass with a piece of shaped ice. (If you do not have an *escanciador*, you can throw (see page 17) the drink in the same way they do in Barcelona and Havana.) Top with the bitters. Return the bottle to the freezer until you are ready for the next round.

OLD FLAME

DIFFICULTY ³
ABV NA
FRUITY, SPICY

When we were working on our stand-alone menu titled the Four Elements, we came up with an idea to lower the acidity of coffee to make a refreshing non-alcoholic drink. Both the pineapple juice and the Baked Lemon Syrup (page 244) in the Old Flame soften the acidity of the Spiced Coffee (page 243), while imparting a tropical air that goes beyond a conventional iced coffee.

100 ml (3½ fl oz) Spiced Coffee (page 243)
30 ml (1 fl oz) Baked Lemon Syrup (page 244)
100 ml (3½ fl oz) pineapple juice
Dried pineapple wheels (see page 235), scorched with a blowtorch, to garnish

Combine the spiced coffee, syrup and pineapple juice in a cocktail shaker filled with ice and shake vigorously until the drink is sufficiently chilled. Strain into a pilsner glass filled with ice and garnish with the scorched pineapple wheels.

OMEGA

DIFFICULTY ²
ABV ¹
SOUR, TANGY

As the last letter of the Greek alphabet, omega has traditionally symbolized a sense of comprehensiveness – of being all that you can be, of being perfect to the end. In modern times, to be an omega person is the opposite of an alpha. Instead of being confident, bold, the first in everything, as an omega you are completely your own person regardless of others' expectations. This Omega is a clear, citrusy take on a Margarita with softer, more complex notes than its bold predecessor. The lightly aged tequila couples well with our house-made Soft Lime Juice (page 235) and mandarin orange bitters, resulting in a sophisticated interpretation. The coriander bitters add a familiar herbal freshness that is characteristic of fine Mexican cuisine.

45 ml (1½ fl oz) reposado tequila
30 ml (1 fl oz) Soft Lime Juice (page 235)
5 ml (1 barspoon) mandarin orange bitters or orange bitters
2 dashes coriander bitters
Red Salty Lime Disc Water Cake (page 236), to garnish

Combine the tequila, soft lime juice, orange bitters and coriander bitters in a mixing glass filled with ice and stir until well chilled. Strain into a rocks glass with a piece of block ice. Garnish with a red salty lime water cake set on top of the ice.

OOPS I DROPPED AN OLIVE

DIFFICULTY ²
ABV ³
HERBAL, SWEET

This cocktail is dedicated to Italian restaurateur and Michelin-starred chef Massimo Bottura, who created his signature dish Oops I Dropped the Lemon Tart after one of his staff dropped a lemon tart. Sometimes when you make a mistake you discover something new. One Christmas when Giorgio was a barback (assistant to the bartender), he added some pine needles to a bottle of gin and left them to infuse overnight to enhance the juniper, but instead found an olive oil character structure similar to the Martini. He was able to fool famous palates from across Italy with this faux olive oil flavour. Massimo even tried it at the bar and loved it. This drink has deep texture and a heady aromatic atmosphere. A day-long infusion of pine needles with the gin lends a surprising aroma of extra virgin olive oil. The Italicus Rosolio di Bergamotto – an Italian liqueur produced from rose petals and bergamot oranges – marries well with vibrant vanilla notes of the Galliano l'Autentico as well as the bitter character of Mediterranean citruses (including chinotto, bergamot, orange, tangerine and grapefruit), juniper, cardamom, lavender and other spices found in the Galliano l'Aperitivo. Garnished with a green olive, the Italian heritage and humour of this Martini-like cocktail will make you smile.

60 ml (2 fl oz) Pine-infused Gin (page 237)
5 ml (1 barspoon) Galliano l'Autentico
5 ml (1 barspoon) Galliano l'Aperitivo
30 ml (1 fl oz) Italicus Rosolio di Bergamotto
Green olive, to garnish

Combine the gin, Galliano l'Autentico, Galliano l'Aperitivo and Italicus Rosolio di Bergamotto in a mixing glass filled with ice and stir until well chilled. Strain into a coupette and garnish with a green olive.

L'ORANGERIE

DIFFICULTY [2]
ABV [1]
SOUR, ORANGEY

A truly elegant vestige of a bygone era, orangeries went beyond being greenhouses. Designed to allow oranges to grow in Britain's chilly and grey weather, they were also frequently used as places for music and light entertainment, spots purely intended for enjoying life's better moments. Our L'Orangerie is a greenhouse of global flavours and beautiful blooms.

30 ml (1 fl oz) cachaça
10 ml (⅓ fl oz) elderflower liqueur
15 ml (½ fl oz) Sea Buckthorn Sherbet (page 242)
30 ml (1 fl oz) kombucha
30 ml (1 fl oz) champagne
Fresh Floregano® (an edible, pale green flower), to garnish

Combine the cachaça, liqueur, sherbet and kombucha in a mixing glass filled with ice and stir until well chilled. Strain into a wooden tumbler over a piece of block ice, top with the champagne and garnish with Floregano® flowers.

PEARENDIPITY

DIFFICULTY ¹
ABV ¹
FRUITY, MINTY

Chance encounters can yield delightful results! The Connaught Bar hosted a week-long 'jam' session in 2014, featuring head bartender Colin Field of the Bar Hemingway in the Ritz Paris Hotel and myself. The Pearendipity is one of the outcomes of our improvised collaboration. While Field's classic Serendipity highlights a marriage of apple juice, Calvados and champagne, this special blend serves up the fun of a Mojito with the sophistication of a champagne cocktail. Crisp, tangy pear meets the tropical influence of the deep, fruity character of dark Cuban rum with its distinctive notes of vanilla, nutmeg, cinnamon and aged wood. This spirituous blend is also complemented with the zesty, citrusy notes of the Lime Sherbet (page 242). Perfumed with the aroma of fresh mint, the Pearendipity delivers a refreshing sip that works with as an aperitif, a refreshing summer drink or as an accompaniment with roasted pork.

100 ml (3½ fl oz) champagne
50 ml (1¾ fl oz) 7-year-old Cuban rum
30 ml (1 fl oz) fresh pear juice
30 ml (1 fl oz) Lime Sherbet (page 242)
10 fresh mint leaves
2 pieces of dried pear (see page 235) and a mint sprig, to garnish

Gently pour the champagne into an ice-filled highball glass. Combine the rum, pear juice and sherbet in a cocktail shaker filled with ice. Slap the mint leaves on the back of your hand and add them to the shaker. Gently shake the mixture so the mint does not release any bitter notes. Double strain into the glass and garnish with the dried pear pieces and a mint sprig.

PRIMO

DIFFICULTY [2]
ABV [1]
MILKY, BITTER

Primo means 'first' in Italian. This drink was inspired by our beautiful pewter-trimmed marble bar top; both powerful and elegant. When you enter, the bar draws your eyes, and it is the first thing you see. The Primo goes far beyond a single note, playing a major chord of spices and classic bitter notes in perfect pitch and harmony. Inspired by the aromas and flavours of Amazonia, the Muyu Chinotto Nero Liqueur introduces cinchona, oak moss, sweet oranges and the bitter chinotto oranges to the mix. The Rubino Vermouth, which revives and enhances a 150-year old vermouth di Torino recipe with rare sandalwood and three types of wormwood, adds complexity. While the rum provides depth, the coconut milk brings a hint of velvet to the mix.

100 ml (1½ fl oz) Primo Coconut Milk Punch (page 240)
30 ml (1 fl oz) grapefruit and rosemary tonic water

Combine the milk punch and tonic water in a mixing glass filled with ice and stir until well chilled. Strain into an old fashioned glass or tumbler over a piece of block ice.

PRISM

DIFFICULTY ³
ABV ¹
SPICY, ALMONDY

A three-dimensional object with two identical sides and equal cross-sections, a prism allows a viewer to see light refract in different directions and reveals a wide range of vibrant colours. Our Prism allows the sipper to experience zesty, spicy, bright flavours with each sip. A non-alcoholic version of our Mystery of Simplicity (page 162), the Prism is a perfect pick-me-up that brings together big flavours from vibrant berries, bright aromatics such as coconut vinegar, lion's mane, caraway, yerba mate, chilli, damiana leaf and cocoa bean in the Everleaf Forest non-alcoholic aperitif, while the Fermented Green Apple (page 234) and an Almond Sherbet (page 242) that features almond and orange blossoms unites the various points in this libation with soft, fruity notes. Finished with a touch of oaky sparkle, the Prism will refresh your perspective on life.

50 ml (1¾ fl oz) Three Spirits Social Elixir
15 ml (½ fl oz) Fermented Green Apple (page 234)
10 ml (⅓ fl oz) Almond Sherbet (page 242)
30 ml (1 fl oz) oakwood tonic water
Fresh blue cornflowers, to garnish

Combine the Three Spirits Social Elixir, fermented green apple, sherbet and tonic water in a mixing glass filled with ice and stir until well chilled. Strain into a Kyoto glass filled with ice and garnish with fresh blue cornflowers set on top of the ice.

RIPPLE

DIFFICULTY ³
ABV NA
FRUITY, CITRUSY

Creativity may start with a single drop. But truly creative expressions make ripples in the fabric of peoples' hearts and minds. What makes this drink cause ripples to the senses is the pairing of our house-made Chicha Morada (page 232) – a South American beverage made with Peruvian purple corn, apples and key limes with hints of cinnamon and clove – and Everleaf Forest, a non-alcoholic aperitif that features woodland botanicals mingled with saffron, vanilla and orange blossom. This intricate fabric of flavours and aromas is trimmed with bright notes of citrus, peach, jasmine and vanilla that cause waves of flavour that capture your imagination with every sip.

45 ml (1½ fl oz) Everleaf Forest
45 ml (1½ fl oz) Chicha Morada (page 232)
20 ml (⅔ fl oz) Clementine and Tonka Bean Shrub (page 243)
50 ml (1¾ fl oz) white peach and jasmine soda
Disc-shaped banana leaf, to garnish

Combine the Everleaf Forest, chicha morada, shrub and soda in a mixing glass filled with ice and stir until well chilled. Strain into a highball glass filled with ice. Garnish with a disc-shaped banana leaf.

RISTRETTO MANHATTAN

DIFFICULTY [1]
ABV [3]
RICH, FRUITY

An iconic drink, the Manhattan is a member of the holy trinity of classic cocktails that includes the Martini and the Daiquirí. While this classic is frequently made with either bourbon or rye whiskey, the inclusion of Italian red vermouth is too sweet for some palates. I created this elegant, grown-up version of a classic Manhattan when I worked at Montgomery Place off Portobello Road in London. I translated the elements of a Manhattan, using bourbon and Punt e Mes vermouth – an aperitif wine whose name literally translates to 'one point' sweetness and a 'half point' bitterness. The first twist comes from the flavour of a traditional Italian pick-me-up – a ristretto or short shot of espresso – from the coffee liqueur. The second twist is the hint of blackberry fruitiness from the crème de mûre. Like the classic Manhattan, my Ristretto Manhattan announces the end of the workday with distinctive flavours that also work as an accompaniment to a mixed grill or a perfectly executed steak.

45 ml (1½ fl oz) bourbon
20 ml (⅔ fl oz) Punt e Mes vermouth
10 ml (⅓ fl oz) dry coffee liqueur
5 ml (1 barspoon) crème de mûre
2 dashes Abbott's Bitters or Angostura Bitters
Spray of orange essence
1 fresh blackberry, to garnish

Combine the bourbon, vermouth, coffee liqueur, crème de mûre and bitters in a mixing glass filled with ice and stir until well chilled. Strain into a red wine glass fitted with an ice sphere. Spray orange essence over the top and garnish with a fresh blackberry tied onto a stirring stick and suspended over the edge of the glass.

ROYAL SEAL

DIFFICULTY ³
ABV ²
SOUR, FRUITY

Why did we name this drink the Royal Seal? To quote the British style publication, *Tatler*: 'Named after Queen Victoria's seventh child Arthur, later Prince Arthur, Duke of Connaught and Strathearn, the Connaught occupies the most majestic spot in Mayfair,... it remains a royal favourite, from the Queen Mother who opened the hotel's new kitchen to its glorious restaurant the Connaught Grill, a restaurant loved by Princess Diana, who would regularly lunch there with her stepmother Countess Raine.' This cocktail is our personal toast to the hotel's royal history and the recognition it has garnered over its long history. It is a drink that is alive with tropical fruits that sing with flavour hints of mango, apricot and coffee.

45 ml (1½ fl oz) reposado tequila
30 ml (1 fl oz) Passion Fruit and Makrut Lime Sherbet (page 242)
10 ml (⅓ fl oz) orange liqueur
10 ml (⅓ fl oz) fresh lime juice
2 dashes Coffee Tincture (page 245)
½ passion fruit, pulp scooped out
Passion fruit slice and a fresh edible flower, to garnish

Combine the tequila, sherbet, liqueur, lime juice, tincture and passion fruit pulp in a cocktail shaker filled with ice and shake vigorously until the drink is sufficiently chilled. Double strain into a coupette and garnish with a passion fruit slice topped with a fresh edible flower.

SANDIA

DIFFICULTY ²
ABV ¹
FRUITY, PIQUANT

A modern classic that follows the same simple pattern as the Martini with gin, the Manhattan with rye and the Sidecar with cognac, the Margarita is the epitome of a tequila cocktail, combining spirit with lime and triple sec. Our Sandia, which means 'watermelon' in Spanish, is a refreshing twist on this cocktail masterpiece. We introduced a Watermelon and Tomato Stalk Shrub (page 243) to our version for complexity. Then we spiced the mixture with Ancho Reyes Chile Liqueur made from poblano chillies and pineapple. And we added a touch of Amaro Santoni, made with thirty-four botanicals, which imparts a long bittersweet aroma of clove and piney freshness.

Neutral spirit, for spraying the glass
Watermelon Rind and Jalapeño Powder (page 242), to decorate the glass
45 ml (1½ fl oz) reposado tequila
45 ml (1½ fl oz) Watermelon and Tomato Stalk Shrub (page 243)
5 ml (1 barspoon) Ancho Reyes Chile Liqueur
10 ml (⅓ fl oz) Amaro Santoni

Spray one side of a coupette with a neutral spirit and dust the same side of the glass with watermelon rind and jalapeño powder with the help of a powder decorating shaker. Combine the tequila, shrub, liqueur and amaro in a mixing glass filled with ice and stir until well chilled. Strain into the prepared coupette.

THE SCENTED CUP

DIFFICULTY [2]
ABV [2]
DRY, AROMATIC

The Scented Cup is a successor to the Corpse Reviver No. 2, a classic created by Harry Craddock when he presided over the American Bar at the Savoy during the 1920s. Here, we replace the lemon juice with dry sherry and infuse the Lillet with floral, earthy saffron for a gentler and far more refined 'reviver'. The cucamelon, a diminutive member of the cucumber family native to Central and South America, contributes hints of sweet cucumber and subtle citrus. The signature dash of absinthe is what makes The Scented Cup a true descendant of Craddock's famed Corpse Reviver family.

30 ml (1 fl oz) London dry gin
30 ml (1 fl oz) Saffron-infused Lillet Blanc (page 237)
20 ml (⅔ fl oz) dry sherry
1 dash absinthe
Cucamelon or a strip of cucumber skin, to garnish

Combine the gin, Lillet Blanc, sherry and absinthe in a mixing glass filled with ice and stir until well chilled. Strain into a tumbler or old fashioned glass over a ball of ice. Garnish with a cucamelon – skewered onto a wooden stick, tied onto a stirring stick and suspended over the edge of the glass – or a strip of cucumber skin.

SET IN STONE

DIFFICULTY ²
ABV ³
DRY, MINERAL

There are many portions of our lives that are malleable like sculptor's clay. There are others that evoke a sense of permanency and from that foundation one can find strength and structure, a place where one can find identity. Set in Stone brings together classic flavours and aromas that are part of the foundation of many familiar cocktails. Gin and genever both offer that sense of tradition and permanency. This solid structure is complemented by other classic ingredients from the cocktail repertoire – rich, luscious sherry plus a waft of bergamot rosolio – plus the aroma of elicriso essence, extracted from *Helichrysum orientale* flowers. Minerality is introduced into the mixture with the stone paper garnish (a paper made from discarded stone), reminding you that the love of a fine cocktail is an element in life that is set in stone.

90 ml (3 fl oz) Set in Stone Mix (page 242)
Piece of stone paper and a green olive, to garnish

Add the Set in Stone mix to a cocktail shaker and shake over ice. Strain into a red wine glass over a piece of block ice and garnish with a piece of stone paper and a green olive.

SIKELIA

DIFFICULTY ²
ABV ¹
CITRUSY, BITTER

Sikelia – the Greek name for the beautiful island of Sicily – was where Giorgio travelled in winter 2022 to visit a blood orange farm situated at the base of a volcano at the height of the growing season. It was there that he was inspired to create this drink, which combines gin, red vermouth and a Pomegranate and Fennel Shrub (page 243) with a sparkling blood orange soda.

50 ml (1¾ fl oz) blood orange soda
30 ml (1 fl oz) London dry gin
20 ml (⅔ fl oz) 1757 vermouth di Torino Rosso
15 ml (½ fl oz) Pomegranate and Fennel Shrub (page 243)
White chocolate disc, to garnish

Pour the blood orange soda into a white wine glass. Combine the gin, vermouth and shrub in a mixing glass filled with ice and stir until well chilled. Strain into the glass. Sink a piece of block ice into the glass and garnish with a disc of white chocolate set on top of the ice.

THE SILKY WAY

DIFFICULTY ²
ABV NA
RICH, FRUITY

Three years after the Tea Rinfresco (page 206) was created, we took a rare step to use one of our own drinks as the inspiration for making another. This time, we married oolong tea with date syrup and a hint of lime to reflect the feeling of looking up at a clear night sky.

50 ml (1¾ fl oz) fresh pear juice
20 ml (⅔ fl oz) Salted Date Syrup (page 245)
20 ml (⅔ fl oz) fresh lime juice
50 ml (1¾ fl oz) brewed oolong tea
Dried pear slices (see page 235), to garnish

Combine the pear juice, syrup, lime juice and tea in a cocktail shaker filled with ice and shake vigorously until the drink is sufficiently chilled. Double strain into a Kyoto glass over ice cubes. Garnish with slices of dried pear set on top of the ice.

SINGAPORE SWIZZLE

DIFFICULTY [2]
ABV [1]
FRUITY, ALMONDY

A quick, efficient tool for giving a drink lift while it diminishes the sparkle of the soda, the original swizzle stick was born during the eighteenth century in the West Indies. Fashioned from a branch of the *Quararibea tubinata*, or 'swizzle stick' tree, this device lent its name to a whole category of drinks that follow this tried-and-true method for mixing. Singapore is the traditional birthplace of the Straits Sling and its fruity modern descendant the Singapore Sling. Our creation combines the best features of this East Indies recipe blended with a West Indies mixing technique. And the herbaceous touch of Bénédictine (a French liqueur made with twenty-seven berries, flowers, herbs and spices) along with ratafia (a similar Italian liqueur made with stone fruit kernels, spices and citrus peel) make for a herbal, spicy and fruity blend highlighted by the tropical freshness of coconut soda that takes this drink far beyond the Singapore Sling to a grown-up, sophisticated level. To make the garnish, we made an ice cup and then crushed it and used an ice stamp to add our design, then added coconut flakes on the top.

45 ml (1½ fl oz) London dry gin
10 ml (⅓ fl oz) Bénédictine
10 ml (⅓ fl oz) ratafia
45 ml (1½ fl oz) fresh pineapple juice
5 ml (1 barspoon) Pomegranate Syrup (page 245)
2 dashes Angostura Bitters
60 ml (2 fl oz) coconut soda
Shaved coconut and a cocktail cherry, to garnish

Combine the gin, Bénédictine, ratafia, pineapple juice, syrup and bitters in a cocktail shaker filled with ice and shake vigorously until the drink is sufficiently chilled. Strain into a pilsner glass and slowly add the coconut soda and more crushed ice. Lift the drink (see page 16). Garnish with a crushed ice cup filled with shaved coconut and a cocktail cherry.

THE SUN OF LONDON

DIFFICULTY 3
ABV 1
SOUR, ORANGEY

Unrelated to the tabloid newspaper with a similar name, The Sun of London is a nod to the Connaught Bar's heritage and the Italian master mixologists who presided behind the bar. This vibrant, bergamot-infused cocktail brings a warm Italian spirit to Mayfair in a swirl of grapefruit and basil essence. It's always sunny in Italy, but in London those halcyon days have always been cause for celebration, especially for Italian bartenders braving the grey to make drinks in the world's best city for cocktail culture and bringing their own sunshine with them in their creations. Podére Santa Bianca Liquore No. 4 is a liqueur with notes of citruses, herb and spices including clementine, cloves and myrtle.

Strip of blood orange fruit leather, to garnish
50 ml (1¾ fl oz) Cocoa Butter and Bergamot Oil-washed Vodka (page 234)
5 ml (1 barspoon) Podére Santa Bianca Liquore No. 4
5 ml (1 barspoon) Italicus Rosolio di Bergamotto
20 ml (⅔ fl oz) Clementine and Tonka Bean Shrub (page 243)
100 ml (3½ fl oz) white peach and jasmine soda
Spray of Podére Santa Bianca Grapefruit and Basil essence

Wrap a strip of blood orange fruit leather around the inside edge of a highball glass and fill the glass with ice to hold the fruit leather in place. Combine the vodka, Podére Santa Bianca Liquore No. 4, Italicus Rosolio di Bergamotto, shrub and soda in a mixing glass filled with ice and stir until well chilled. Strain into the prepared glass. Spray with the essence and garnish with a strip of blood orange fruit leather.

SWEET AND Z

DIFFICULTY [2]
ABV [1]
CHOCOLATY, BITTER

This drink is named after two of our most regular guests. Originally from Milan, Mr Sweet works in the cinema industry, travelling the globe throughout the year. He typically orders a dry Martini, Negroni or Margarita. Mr Z works in the pharmaceutical industry, commuting regularly from Milan to London. He likes fruity, lighter drinks, like a Cosmopolitan, or creamier cocktails, such as Grasshoppers and Brandy Alexanders. Friends for nearly twenty years, the only time they get to meet and catch up is at our bar. Even visually, they are like night and day. So, we decided to make a drink that honours them both: it is an herbaceous, chocolaty concoction that satisfies people with both types of palates. Combining the strong herbal traits of a Negroni, made with tequila, bitter aperitif and vermouth, with a Golden Cadillac, crafted from a vanilla-based Italian liqueur, cacao nibs and cream, this clarified milk punch makes the perfect party drink since it can be batched, chilled over ice and finished with a light spray of essential oil and a piece of chocolate.

90 ml (3 fl oz) Sweet and Z Milk Punch (page 241)
Spray of grapefruit and basil food-grade essential oil
Green-tinted chocolate ring, to garnish

Combine the milk punch in a mixing glass filled with ice and stir until well chilled. Strain into a coupette with a piece of shaped ice – the ice is shaped with two presses: the bottom of a diamond ice press and the top of a sphere ice press. Spray the top with the essential oil and garnish with a ring of green-tinted chocolate.

TEA RINFRESCO

DIFFICULTY ²
ABV NA
FRUITY, SPICY

In its name, tea, Britain's most popular and iconic beverage, meets the Italian phrase: 'I refresh you'. Brits are famed around the world for their passion for a cuppa, Italians for their capacity to be hospitable. There are so many more dimensions than milk and two sugars to explore and this light, zesty drink refreshes in a way all its own. Here, jasmine tea is given eastern accents with ginger syrup, lemon juice and pear.

40 ml (1⅓ fl oz) pear juice
20 ml (⅔ fl oz) Ginger Syrup (page 244)
20 ml (⅔ fl oz) fresh lemon juice
30 ml (1 fl oz) brewed jasmine tea
Dried pear slice (see page 235) and a mint sprig, to garnish

Combine the pear juice, syrup, lemon juice and tea in a cocktail shaker filled with ice and shake vigorously until the drink is sufficiently chilled. Double strain into a highball glass over ice cubes. Garnish with a dried pear slice and a mint sprig.

TIP OF THE ICEBERG

DIFFICULTY ²
ABV ²
CHOCOLATY, FRUITY

The clear waters of the Mediterranean Sea on a summer afternoon evoke zesty and herbaceous aromas. Waves of flavours that harken from southern Italy, the Greek Islands and Corsica remind you there is more to each sip of this delicately crafted balance of grappa-based cedro lemon liqueur, crème de cacao and coconut water that complements the exotic notes that arise from the Banana and Coconut Oil-washed Gin (page 233). With the first sip, you will understand that you are only experiencing the tip of an iceberg.

50 ml (1¾ fl oz) Banana and Coconut Oil-washed Gin (page 233)
20 ml (⅔ fl oz) crème de cacao
10 ml (⅓ fl oz) cedro lemon liqueur
20 ml (⅔ fl oz) coconut water
Blue Disc Water Cake (page 235), to garnish

Combine the gin, crème de cacao, liqueur and coconut water in a mixing glass filled with ice and stir until well chilled. Strain into a coupette with a piece of shaped ice and garnish with a blue disc water cake.

UNDER A STONE

DIFFICULTY [3]
ABV [2]
NUTTY, SAVOURY

Under a Stone was included in our stand-alone menu titled the Four Elements. Earth, wind, fire and water were represented in this drinks list. A twist on the Martinez, this drink portrays its earthy tones thanks to the Truffle Butter-washed Vodka (page 234) and Wattleseed-infused Vermouth (page 238). Harvested from Australian acacia trees, wattleseeds impart a nutty, roasted coffee aroma that tastes like a toasted wheat biscuit. Then truffle and coffee take the starring role in both the palate and the nose from the first sip to the last.

30 ml (1 fl oz) Truffle Butter-washed Vodka (page 234)
60 ml (2 fl oz) Wattleseed-infused Vermouth (page 238)
2 dashes Aphrodite Bitters
5 ml (1 barspoon) maraschino liqueur
2 chocolate stones, to garnish

Combine the vodka, vermouth, bitters and liqueur in a mixing glass filled with ice and stir until well chilled. Strain into a chilled coupette and garnish with two chocolate stones.

UNVEILED

DIFFICULTY ²
ABV ²
FRUITY, MILKY

Voila! The levels of anticipation and excitement that exhilarate the senses when a masterpiece is unveiled defy all expectations. This was the idea behind the marriage of the ceramic tumbler crafted by Japanese ceramicist Reiko Kaneko with the rum and pineapple cocktail drink we created as its accompaniment. We pour the Unveiled into its unique vessel in front of the customer. The tumbler's dark, smoky exterior belies the tastes found on the inside: a bold, heady blend of pineapple-infused cognac and aged Jamaican rum with warm cardamom and coffee notes.

2 drops cardamom bitters
20 ml (¾ fl oz) cognac
90 ml (3 fl oz) Coffee and Pineapple Milk Punch (page 240)

Add the bitters to the bottom of a ceramic tumbler. Combine the cognac and milk punch in a mixing glass filled with ice and stir until well chilled. Strain into the prepared tumbler over a piece of block ice.

VELVET CHAMPAGNE

DIFFICULTY [1]
ABV [1]
SWEET, CREAMY

Champagne's bubbly nature contributes vigour to this twist on a Soyer au Champagne, which was one of Queen Victoria's favourite libations. This ice cream cocktail is named after Alexis Benoît Soyer – London's first and foremost Victorian celebrity chef. The head chef at the private members' establishment the Reform Club when it first opened its doors in 1836, Soyer's talents shined outside the kitchen and into the bar as he also created lake blue sparkling drinks, punch jellies and this clever ice cream confection. Our Velvet Champagne is less sweet and fruitier than its predecessor, allowing every sip of cream and champagne to sing on its own.

20 ml (⅔ fl oz) framboise eau-de-vie
20 ml (⅔ fl oz) orange cognac liqueur
5 ml (1 barspoon) Sugar Syrup (page 245)
10 ml (⅓ fl oz) fresh lemon juice
20 ml (⅔ fl oz) raspberry purée
30 ml (1 fl oz) champagne
1 small scoop good-quality vanilla ice cream, preferably French

Combine the eau-de-vie, liqueur, sugar syrup, lemon juice and purée in a cocktail shaker filled with ice and shake vigorously until the drink is sufficiently chilled. Strain into a copper-plated Moscow mule mug filled with a piece of block ice. Top with the champagne, then float a scoop of vanilla ice cream on the surface of the ice. Lift to blend (see page 16) and serve with a spoon for the ice cream.

VERIZON

DIFFICULTY [2]
ABV [2]
SOUR, FRUITY

While the name of this drink combines the Latin term for 'truth' – *veritas* – with the word 'horizon', a blazing summer sunset invites you to reflect on the hopes and dreams that lay just over the horizon. The truth of this meditation can be found in the meeting of whisky's smoky character and champagne's light hints of toast. With tangy and tropical notes of rhubarb and mango, the Verizon is the perfect sip served with a piece of dark chocolate on the side for a sultry, summer moment of contemplation as the sun sets.

30 ml (1 fl oz) Scotch whisky
50 ml (1¾ fl oz) Rhubarb and Mango Cordial (page 233)
100 ml (3½ fl oz) champagne
Golden grape (a grape painted with edible golden paint and left to dry), to garnish

Combine the whisky, cordial and champagne in a mixing glass filled with ice. Stir lightly and strain into a highball glass filled with ice. Garnish with a golden grape skewered onto a cocktail pick.

VIEUX CONNAUGHT

DIFFICULTY ²
ABV ³
WOODY, SMOKY

A delicate waft of saffron smoke caresses the rich flavours of rum and rye whiskey in the Vieux Connaught. Inspired by the signature Vieux Carré cocktail created in 1938 by head bartender Walter Bergeron at the Monteleone Hotel in New Orleans, the Vieux Connaught offers a balanced, modern experience. A buttery sweet Guatemalan rum instead of the vanilla and stone fruit character of cognac pairs with the spicy, peppery rye whiskey, softening the woody notes of the spirits. (If you cannot find a Guatemalan rum, you can try a Venezuelan or other solera-style aged Spanish rum.) The flavour is enhanced by silky, honeyed notes, cardamom, nutmeg, cedarwood, sage and citrus peel from the Bénédictine liqueur and it complements the dry, light mineral accents of the Connaught's proprietary dry vermouth. Instead of the intense spiciness from anise, cinnamon, cloves, cherry, plum and blackcurrants found in Peychaud's Bitters, citrusy edges are introduced with dashes of Angostura and orange bitters. The mixture is built and poured into a glass decanter. Next, we smoke the drink by placing a pinch of saffron into a smoking gun and injecting the smoke directly into the decanter. Served on a mirrored tray, the customer can glimpse a rare sight – the bar's elegantly carved ceiling – as the Vieux Connaught is poured from the bottle into a chilled old fashioned glass. The smokiness is controlled to taste by leaving the drink in the smoked decanter for longer if desired. It is an ideal digestif and an excellent accompaniment with smoked salmon, smoked trout or a creamy cheese.

30 ml (1 fl oz) aged Guatemalan rum
20 ml (⅔ fl oz) rye whiskey
20 ml (⅔ fl oz) Connaught Bar Dry Vermouth Mix (page 241)
10 ml (⅓ fl oz) Bénédictine
2 dashes Angostura Bitters
2 dashes orange bitters
Pinch of saffron threads
Z-shaped orange twist, to garnish

Pour the rum, whiskey, vermouth, Bénédictine and bitters into a small glass decanter. Smoke the contents with a pinch of saffron placed into a smoking gun. Inject the smoke directly into the decanter and seal to retain the smoke. To serve, pour about half the drink into an old fashioned glass filled with a piece of block ice and garnish with a z-shaped orange twist. If you do not have a smoking gun, place a pinch of saffron threads on a heatproof plate. Light the threads with a small torch next to the drink-filled old fashioned glass. Immediately place a glass bowl or cloche over the drink and wait for a few moments. Uncover, add a piece of block ice and serve.

VORONOI

DIFFICULTY ²
ABV ¹
SPICY, SOUR

This cocktail is named after the Ukrainian mathematician Georgy Voronoi, who devised the elegant Voronoi diagram that partitions a two-dimensional Euclidean plane into regions, each of a given set of objects. The light floral notes of the tequila, mescal and Lime Sherbet (page 242) contrast yet unite with the earthy, balsamic aromas of the vetiver liqueur, which is made from the vetiver grass, native to India. A subtle touch of nutmeg emanates from the vermouth infused with mace blades – the sister spice of the nutmeg tree. Together these ingredients present a delicate interpretation of how seemingly different elements unite, even though they are not symmetrical.

Edible red and white paint, to decorate the glass
20 ml (⅔ fl oz) blanco tequila
10 ml (⅓ fl oz) mescal
15 ml (½ fl oz) Muyu Vetiver Gris Liqueur
30 ml (1 fl oz) Mace-infused Cocchi Rosa (page 237)
25 ml (¾ fl oz) Lime Sherbet (page 242)

Decorate a coupette with edible red and white paint dots and set aside. Combine the tequila, mescal, liqueur, Cocchi Rosa and sherbet in a cocktail shaker filled with ice and shake vigorously until the drink is sufficiently chilled. Strain into the prepared coupette.

WAYFARER

DIFFICULTY ²
ABV NA
SWEET, FRUITY

For some of our customers, the Connaught Bar is a place of pilgrimage. For others, it is a haven – a home away from home. Whatever your personal voyage, this combination of non-alcoholic botanical spirit, soft berries and sparkling flowers and fruit serves as a tribute to the traveller in all of us. Spicy juniper undertones balance with refreshing eucalyptus, bright citrus and a touch of fiery heat transport you to a surprisingly piney finish.

Edible blue cocoa paint, to decorate the glass
45 ml (1½ fl oz) Sipsmith FreeGlider
45 ml (1½ fl oz) Clarified Berries Yogurt (page 232)
10 ml (⅓ fl oz) Sugar Syrup (page 245)
30 ml (1 fl oz) white peach and jasmine soda

Decorate an old fashioned glass with two stripes of blue edible cocoa paint and set aside. Combine the Sipsmith FreeGlider, yogurt, sugar syrup and soda in a mixing glass filled with ice and stir until well chilled. Strain into the prepared old fashioned over a piece of block ice.

WINE FOR SOUL

DIFFICULTY³
ABV NA
SPICY, RICH

Before there was a non-alcoholic vermouth on the market, we removed the alcohol of the ambrato vermouth with the help of heat from a Thermomix® to create our own non-alcoholic drink. It was our first non-alcoholic drink to make the masterpieces section of our menu. It is a drink of surprises, as the chillies distilled with the vermouth offer flavour but none of the heat, recreating the sensation of alcohol.

45 ml (1½ fl oz) Vietnamese Pepper Evaporated Ambrato (page 243)
30 ml (1 fl oz) Martini Vibranti
15 ml (½ fl oz) Black Cardamom Seed Syrup (page 244)
15 ml (½ fl oz) Riesling Verjus Cordial
60 ml (2 fl oz) soda water
Lemon twist, to garnish

Combine the ambrato, Martini Vibranti, syrup and cordial in a mixing glass filled with ice and stir until well chilled. Strain into a highball glass over ice. Top with the soda water and garnish with a lemon twist.

WOOD

DIFFICULTY ²
ABV ¹
WOODY, BITTER

A drink inspired by the element of wood, this libation takes its cue from the silver and gold tones of the Connaught Bar's wood panelling. Sometimes the greatest inspiration is right before your eyes. In this case, the depth of warm brown tones in the Connaught Bar's wood panelling gave birth to this wonderfully spicy and complex aperitif. Wild cherry bark and catuaba bark convey the message beautifully among the dark, aged spirit and coffee flavours joining together into a deep, warming statement. The grapefruit and rosemary tonic water brings the portrait to life with a zesty sparkle.

Edible white cocoa paint, to decorate the glass
30 ml (1 fl oz) Wild Cherry Bark-infused Pisco (page 238)
10 ml (⅓ fl oz) aged Cuban rum
10 ml (⅓ fl oz) Martini Riserva Speciale Bitter
45 ml (1½ fl oz) Cocchi Americano
10 ml (⅓ fl oz) Catuaba Bark Syrup (page 244)
5 ml (1 barspoon) Italian espresso liqueur
90 ml (3 fl oz) grapefruit and rosemary tonic water

Decorate a highball glass with a stripe of edible white cocoa paint and set aside. Combine the pisco, rum, Martini Riserva Speciale Bitter, Cocchi Americano, syrup and Italian espresso liqueur in a mixing glass filled with ice and stir until well chilled. Strain into a highball glass over ice and top with the tonic water.

YELLOW SUBMARINE

DIFFICULTY [1]
ABV [3]
DRY, HERBAL

Born and raised in Italy, I acquired a passion for the Negroni early in my drinking life. This Italian classic combines herbaceous and bitter notes and is traditionally served during aperitivo – a moment at the end of the workday when conversation and a small bite go hand in hand with this classic refreshment. I created the Yellow Submarine when I first arrived in London in 2006 as the head bartender at Montgomery Place – a bar off Portobello Road. This twist on the Negroni is served like its predecessor, on the rocks, but I use an ice ball instead of cubes. In my version, gin is accentuated by the minerality of sherry, the smooth floral notes of lavender with hints of sweetness from vanilla and anise. Why did I name this drink after a famous song performed by The Beatles? Since I serve this drink on the rocks just like a Negroni, the ice ball, which keeps the drink icy cold, reminds me of a porthole on a submarine. And the drink's pale-yellow hue made it a natural fit to its pop culture name.

50 ml (1¾ fl oz) London dry gin
25 ml (¾ fl oz) fino dry sherry
15 ml (½ fl oz) Galliano l'Autentico
2 dashes celery bitters
Lemon twist and a strip of cucumber skin, to garnish

Combine the gin, sherry, Galliano l'Autentico and bitters in a mixing glass filled with ice and stir until well chilled. Strain and serve in a rocks glass with an ice ball. Squeeze the lemon twist over the drink to express the citrus oils, then garnish with a strip of cucumber skin skewered onto a wooden stick.

HOMEMADE INGREDIENTS

There are a few things to remember when you make one of these 'custom' elements. For example, syrups that include fresh ingredients have a shelf life of no more than three days, while syrups that include essential oils will last for about one week. Milk punches will last about one week if kept refrigerated. Infused and fat-washed spirits will maintain potency for about one month. So, if you plan on making a few drinks with special ingredients, think about cutting the recipe in half, or even by a quarter, to prevent waste.

Because we make cocktails in volume and need to make them quickly, we have some high-end equipment at the Connaught Bar. However, you can accomplish the same results at home with regular utensils and appliances.

To replicate a SOUS-VIDE BAG, place your ingredients in a plastic resealable bag. Instead of a SOUS-VIDE BATH, immerse the plastic resealable bag in a large saucepan filled with enough water to cover the contents of the bag and set the saucepan on a hob (stovetop) that allows you to incrementally control the heat at a low and steady temperature, following the timing and temperature guidance provided in the recipe.

If you don't have a THERMOMIX®, you can heat mixtures in a large saucepan fitted with a digital thermometer to control the heat, following the directions in the recipe. Then pour the heated mixture into a blender to finish.

An ULTRASOUND MACHINE, also known as an ultrasonic homogenizer, allows us to rapidly infuse drinks with new flavours, blend emulsions and age spirits quickly. An ultrasonic jewellery cleaning bath can be used to achieve the same effect. Both these machines are mostly used by professionals. To replicate the process at home, place the ingredients in a sous-vide vacuum bag (or plastic resealable bag) and seal, then cook in a sous-vide bath (see above for alternative options) at 30°C (85°F) for 2 hours.

When working with fresh ingredients for homemade preparations we cannot always predict how it will taste and how easily it will perish, so it is important to always taste the preparations before serving them.

CHICHA MORADA

CHICHA MORADA
- 1.5 litres (50 fl oz) still mineral water
- 250 g (9 oz) sweetcorn kernels
- ½ cinnamon stick
- 2 cloves
- Juice and skins of 4 limes
- 3 green apples, skin on and roughly chopped
- Rind of 6 pineapple wheels
- 200 g (7 oz/1 cup) caster (superfine) sugar

Combine the mineral water, sweetcorn kernels and spices in a Thermomix® (see page 230 for alternative options). Cook at a medium heat until its volume is reduced by half. Pour the mixture into a container and add the lime juice and skins, apples and pineapple rinds. Leave to cool to room temperature. Once cooled, strain the liquid through a chinois or fine-mesh sieve into a bowl, discarding the sweetcorn, spices and fruit. Add the sugar and stir until dissolved. Pour into a 700 ml (24 fl oz) sterilized bottle (see page 256), label and store in the refrigerator for up to 3 days.

CLARIFIED

CLARIFIED BERRIES YOGURT
- 750 g (1 lb 10 oz/3 ⅓ cups) full-fat (whole) Greek yogurt
- 250 ml (8 fl oz) full-fat (whole) milk
- 100 ml (3½ fl oz) strawberry purée
- 100 ml (3½ fl oz) raspberry purée
- 250 ml (8 fl oz) fresh lemon juice
- 250 g (9 oz/ 1¼ cups) caster (superfine) sugar

Add the yogurt, milk and purées to a blender and blend at high speed for 10 seconds. Pour the lemon juice into the blender and blitz again. Leave the mixture to rest for 30 minutes, then strain through a paper coffee filter into a large jug (pitcher). Add the sugar, stir until dissolved, then pour into a 700 ml (24 fl oz) sterilized bottle (see page 256). Label and store in the refrigerator for up to 3 days.

CLARIFIED COFFEE MILK
- 200 ml (7 fl oz) fresh pineapple juice
- 25 g (1 oz) caster (superfine) sugar
- 30 ml (1 fl oz) brewed espresso
- 300 ml (10 fl oz) full-fat (whole) milk

Add all the ingredients, except the milk, to a large container and mix well. Pour in the milk, stir quickly to mix again. Once the mixture starts to split, strain through a paper coffee filter into a 700 ml (24 fl oz) sterilized bottle (see page 256). Label and store in the refrigerator for up to 1 week.

CLARIFIED GRAPEFRUIT JUICE
- 1.5 litres (50 fl oz) fine-strained pink grapefruit juice, at room temperature
- 4 g (2 teaspoons) agar agar powder

Mix 500 ml (17 fl oz) grapefruit juice and the agar agar in a Thermomix® (see page 230 for alternative options) at level 5 speed for a few minutes. Cook for 10 minutes at 100°C (212°F), bringing the mixture to the boiling point. When it reaches the boiling point, slowly pour in the remaining grapefruit juice, keeping the Thermomix® on level 5 speed. Remove and leave to rest in a large container filled with ice cubes for 30 minutes. Fine strain through a muslin cloth (cheesecloth) into a 700 ml (24 fl oz) sterilized bottle (see page 256). Label and store in the refrigerator for up to 3 days.

CLARIFIED PINEAPPLE JUICE
- 1.5 litres (50 fl oz) fine-strained pineapple juice
- 5 g (⅛ oz) agar agar powder

Mix the pineapple juice and agar agar in a Thermomix® (see page 230 for alternative options) at level 5 speed at 100°C (212°F) for 1½ minutes, then reduce the speed to 0.5 and cook for 13½ minutes. Remove and leave the mixture to rest in a large container filled with ice cubes for 30 minutes. Strain through a paper coffee filter into a 700 ml (24 fl oz) sterilized bottle (see page 256). Label and store in the refrigerator for up to 3 days.

CLARIFIED VANILLA MILK
- 100 ml (3½ fl oz) Sugar Syrup (page 245)
- 300 ml (10 fl oz) almond milk
- 100 ml (3½ fl oz) double (heavy) cream
- 100 ml (3½ fl oz) Armagnac
- 10 ml (⅓ fl oz) vanilla extract

- ¼ tonka bean (see page 256), grated
- 30 ml (1 fl oz) fresh lemon juice

Bring the syrup, almond milk, cream, Armagnac, vanilla extract and tonka bean to the boil in a large saucepan. Remove from the heat and add the lemon juice. Leave to infuse for 20 minutes, then strain through a paper coffee filter into a 700 ml (24 fl oz) sterilized bottle (see page 256). Label and store in the refrigerator for up to 1 week.

CLARIFIED WHITE PEACH PURÉE
- 750 ml (25 fl oz) peach purée
- 500 ml (17 fl oz) still mineral water
- 3.75 g (¾ teaspoon) agar agar powder

Pour the peach purée into a large container. Add the mineral water and agar agar to a Thermomix® (see page 230 for alternative options) and mix until dissolved. Increase the temperature to maximum heat and minimum speed until it begins to boil, then remove and pour the mixture into the container with the peach purée and mix well. Place the container in a larger container filled with ice cubes and leave to cool. Once the liquid thickens, strain through a paper coffee filter into a 700 ml (24 fl oz) sterilized bottle (see page 256). Label and store in the refrigerator for up to 3 days.

CORDIALS

BEE BALM AND CASSIA CORDIAL
- 500 ml (17½ fl oz) Sugar Syrup (page 245)
- 250 ml (8 fl oz) still mineral water
- 15 g (½ oz) bee balm leaves
- 10 g (¼ oz) cassia buds

Blitz the syrup, mineral water, bee balm and cassia buds in a Thermomix® (see page 230 for alternative options) at full speed, then reduce the speed and cook the mixture at 40°C (104°F) for 20 minutes. Strain through a paper coffee filter into a 700 ml (24 fl oz) sterilized bottle (see page 256). Label and store in the refrigerator for up to 1 week.

BEETROOT AND BLACKBERRY CORDIAL
- 450 g (1 lb) beetroot
- 750 ml (25 fl oz) still mineral water

- 10 blackberries
- 750 g (1 lb 10 oz/ 3¾ cups) caster (superfine) sugar
- Juice and skins of 2 limes
- 10 ml (⅓ fl oz) citric acid
- 7 lemon thyme sprigs

Pour the beetroot, mineral water, blackberries, sugar and the juice and skins of the limes into a Thermomix® (see page 230 for alternative options). Cook at 85°C (185°F) for 50 minutes. When finished, add the citric acid and lemon thyme. Stir and cool. Fine strain through a muslin cloth (cheesecloth) into a 700 ml (24 fl oz) sterilized bottle (see page 256). Label and store in the refrigerator for up to 1 week.

RHUBARB AND MANGO CORDIAL
- 300 g (11 oz) fresh rhubarb, diced
- 300 g (11 oz) fresh mango, diced
- 1 kg (2 ¼ lb/5 cups) caster (superfine) sugar
- 1.5 litres (50 fl oz) water
- 1 vanilla pod (bean)

Place the rhubarb, mango, sugar and water into a Thermomix® (see page 230 for alternative options). Bring to the boil, then simmer for 10 minutes. Switch off the heat. Add the vanilla pod to the liquid and leave to infuse until the mixture has cooled. Strain through a paper coffee filter into a 700 ml (24 fl oz) sterilized bottle (see page 256). Label and store in the refrigerator for up to 3 days.

RHUBARB AND RED FRUITS CORDIAL
- 300 g (11 oz) fresh rhubarb, diced
- 1 kg (2¼ lb/5 cups) caster (superfine) sugar
- 10 fresh strawberries
- 10 fresh raspberries
- 1.5 litres (50 fl oz) still mineral water
- 1 vanilla pod (bean)

Bring the rhubarb, sugar, strawberries, raspberries and mineral water to the boil in a saucepan, then simmer for 10 minutes. Remove from the heat, add the vanilla pod (bean) and leave to cool. Strain through a paper coffee filter into a 700 ml (24 fl oz) sterilized bottle (see page 256). Label and store in the refrigerator for up to 5 days.

FAT-WASHED SPIRITS

BANANA AND COCONUT OIL-WASHED GIN
- 175 g (6 oz) dried banana (see page 235)
- 500 g (1 lb 2 oz) coconut oil, melted
- 750 ml (25 fl oz) gin

Place the dried banana and melted coconut oil in a sous-vide vacuum bag (or plastic resealable bag) and seal. Cook in a sous-vide bath (see page 230 for alternative options) at 70°C (170°F) for 4 hours. Take 250 g (9 oz) of the banana and oil mixture and mix it into the bottle of gin. Leave to steep for 30 minutes, then freeze the bottle until the coconut oil becomes solid. Remove the solid portion and fine strain through a muslin cloth (cheesecloth) into a 700 ml (24 fl oz) sterilized bottle (see page 256). Label and store at room temperature for up to 1 month.

COCONUT OIL-WASHED PUERTO RICAN RUM
- 500 ml (17 fl oz) blended Caribbean rum
- 250 ml (8 fl oz) Puerto Rican rum
- 175 ml (6 fl oz) coconut oil

Place the rums and oil in a sous-vide vacuum bag (or plastic resealable bag) and seal. Cook in a sous-vide bath (see page 230 for alternative options) at 60°C (140°F) for 1 hour. Pour the mixture into a large freezerproof container and freeze for 24 hours. The mixture will have separated, so remove the solid portion from the container and strain the liquid through a paper coffee filter into a 700 ml (24 fl oz) sterilized bottle (see page 256). Label and store in the refrigerator for up to 1 month.

ALMOND AND PEANUT BUTTERS-WASHED REPOSADO TEQUILA
- 100 g (3½ oz) almond butter
- 100 g (3½ oz) peanut butter
- 1 litre (34 fl oz) grapeseed oil
- 1 litre (34 fl oz) resposado tequila

Melt the almond and peanut butters in the grapeseed oil in a large saucepan over a low heat. Remove from the heat, pour the mixture into a large freezerproof container and add the tequila. Leave to infuse for 3 hours. Transfer the mixture to the freezer until the oil solidifies. Remove the solid portion from the container and strain the liquid through a paper coffee filter into a 700 ml (24 fl oz) sterilized bottle (see page 256). Label and store in the refrigerator for up to 1 month.

TOASTED SESAME OIL-WASHED BLANCO TEQUILA

- 700 ml (24 fl oz) blanco tequila
- 50 ml (1¾ fl oz) toasted sesame oil

Mix the tequila and sesame oil in a large freezerproof container and freeze for 24 hours. Fine strain through a paper coffee filter into a 700 ml (24 fl oz) sterilized bottle (see page 256). Label and store in the refrigerator for up to 1 month.

WALNUT OIL-WASHED REPOSADO TEQUILA

- 700 ml (24 fl oz) reposado tequila
- 100 ml (3½ fl oz) walnut oil

Place the tequila and oil in a large freezerproof container. Give the mixture a quick stir. Leave to infuse for 2 hours, then freeze for 24 hours. Strain through a paper coffee filter into a 700 ml (24 fl oz) sterilized bottle (see page 256). Label and store in the refrigerator for up to 1 month.

BERRY AND GRAPESEED OIL-WASHED VODKA AND GIN

- 100 ml (3½ fl oz) grapeseed oil
- 150 ml (5 fl oz) strawberry purée
- 150 ml (5 fl oz) raspberry purée
- 5 g (⅛ oz) sea salt
- 2 g (¹⁄₁₀ oz) peppercorns
- 350 ml (12 fl oz) Japanese gin
- 350 ml (12 fl oz) Japanese vodka
- 60 ml (2 fl oz) crème de violette

Mix the oil, strawberry purée, raspberry purée, salt and peppercorns in a blender at high speed for 10 seconds. Pour into a large freezerproof container, add the gin, vodka and crème de violette and freeze for 24 hours. Strain through a paper coffee filter into a 700 ml (24 fl oz) sterilized bottle (see page 256). Label and store in the refrigerator for up to 1 month.

COCOA BUTTER-WASHED VODKA

- 200 g (7 oz) cocoa butter
- 700 ml (24 fl oz) vodka

Place the cocoa butter in a heatproof bowl set over a saucepan of gently simmering water, making sure that the bottom of the bowl doesn't touch the water, and leave until melted. Remove the bowl from the pan, add the vodka and leave to steep for 2 hours. Pour the mixture into a large freezerproof container and freeze for 24 hours. Once the mixture is completely separated, remove the solid portion from the container and strain the liquid through a paper coffee filter into a 700 ml (24 fl oz) sterilized bottle (see page 256). Label and store at room temperature for up to 1 month.

COCOA BUTTER AND BERGAMOT OIL-WASHED VODKA

- 200 g (7 oz) cocoa butter
- 2 drops bergamot food-grade essential oil
- 700 ml (24 fl oz) vodka

Place the cocoa butter in a heatproof bowl set over a saucepan of gently simmering water, making sure that the bottom of the bowl doesn't touch the water, and leave until melted. Transfer the melted cocoa butter to a large freezerproof container, add the bergamot oil and stir until well mixed. Add the vodka and stir again until well mixed. Leave to infuse for 2 hours, then freeze for 24 hours. Once completely separated, remove the solid portion from the container strain the liquid through a paper coffee filter into a 700 ml (24 fl oz) sterilized bottle (see page 256). Label and store at room temperature for up to 1 month.

PASSION BERRY AND GRAPESEED OIL-WASHED VODKA

- 100 ml (3½ fl oz) grapeseed oil
- 3 passion fruit seeds
- 7 g (¼ oz) Ethiopian passion berries
- 750 ml (25 fl oz) vodka

Place the grapeseed oil, passion fruit seeds and passion berries in a sous-vide vacuum bag (or plastic resealable bag) and seal. Cook in a sous-vide bath (see page 230 for alternative options) for 4 hours at 70°C (158°F). Strain the mixture into a large freezerproof container along with the vodka. Leave to infuse for 30 minutes, then freeze until the oil solidifies. Fine strain through a muslin cloth (cheesecloth) into a 700 ml

(24 fl oz) sterilized bottle (see page 256). Label and store at room temperature for up to 1 month.

TRUFFLE BUTTER-WASHED VODKA

- 20 g (¾ oz) truffle butter
- 700 ml (24 fl oz) vodka

Place the truffle butter in a small heatproof bowl set over a saucepan of gently simmering water, making sure the bottom of the bowl doesn't touch the water, and leave until melted. Mix the melted butter with the vodka in a large freezerproof container and leave to infuse for 20 minutes, then freeze for 12 hours, or until the butter solidifies. Remove the solid portion from the container and fine strain through a muslin cloth (cheesecloth) into a 700 ml (24 fl oz) sterilized bottle (see page 256). Label and store in the refrigerator for up to 1 month.

FERMENTS

FERMENTED GREEN APPLE

- 500 g (17½ oz) green apples, chopped (you don't need to peel or core them)
- 200 g (7 oz/1 cup) caster (superfine) sugar
- 400 ml (14 fl oz) still mineral water
- 4 g (1 scant teaspoon) salt

Place the apples and sugar in a saucepan and cook over a low-medium heat until the sugar has caramelized on the apples. Place the cooked apples, mineral water and salt into a sous-vide vacuum bag (or plastic resealable bag) and seal. Store it in a warm place away from direct sunlight. Check every day. If the bag inflates too much, transfer the contents to a new bag and seal. The fermentation should be ready in 5–7 days. Transfer to a 700 ml (24 fl oz) sterilized bottle (see page 256) or clean sous-vide bag and store in the refrigerator for up to 3 days.

LACTO-FERMENTED MELON

- 400 g (14 oz/ 1¾ cups) honey
- 4.5 g (1 teaspoon) salt
- 400 ml (14 fl oz) still mineral water
- 500 g (1 lb 2 oz) ripe honeydew melon, peeled and roughly chopped

Place the honey, salt and mineral water in a large container and mix well until dissolved. Add the melon and the honey mixture to a sous-vide vacuum bag (or plastic resealable bag) and seal. Store it in a warm place away from direct sunlight. Check every day. If the bag inflates too much, transfer the contents to a new bag. The fermentation will be ready in 5–7 days. Transfer to a 700 ml (24 fl oz) sterilized bottle (see page 256) or clean sous-vide bag and store in the refrigerator for up to 3 days.

FOAMS

APRICOT VELVET
- 300 ml (10 fl oz) apricot liqueur
- 100 ml (3½ fl oz) still mineral water
- 100 ml (3½ fl oz) Sugar Syrup (page 245)
- 2.5 g (½ teaspoon) sucrose ester powder

Blend the apricot liqueur, mineral water, sugar syrup and sucrose ester in a tall stainless-steel container with a hand-held blender. Pour into an airtight 500 ml (17 fl oz) container, label and store in the refrigerator for up to 1 month. To use, blend the surface to create a foam, then pour the foam onto a spoon and place on top of the cocktail.

CELERY AIR
- 500 ml (17 fl oz) fresh celery juice
- 10 g (¼ oz) lecithin
- 5 g (⅛ oz) celery salt

Place the celery juice, lecithin and celery salt in a blender and mix for a few seconds. Pour into a 500 ml (17 fl oz) sterilized bottle (see page 256). Label and store in the refrigerator for up to 1 day.

FRUITS

BURNT GRAPEFRUIT PEEL
- Peels from 2 pink grapefruits and 2 white grapefruits (set aside the peeled grapefruits to make Grilled Pink and White Grapefruit Juice, see right)

Use a cook's blowtorch to caramelize the grapefruit peels. Label and store the refrigerator for up to 2 days.

BURNT LEMON PEEL
- 2 or 3 lemons
- 5 g (⅛ oz) bamboo charcoal

Preheat the oven to 50°C/122°F/ lowest possible Gas Mark. Peel the lemons, trying to get as little pith on the rinds as possible, then spread them out on a large baking sheet and leave in the oven for 12 hours, or until dried. Once dried, use a cook's blowtorch to caramelize them. Transfer the rinds to a blender, add the charcoal and blitz until ground. Label and store in an airtight container at room temperature for up to 1 month

DRIED FRUIT
You can easily dehydrate slices of fruit at home. Preheat the oven to 50°C/122°F/lowest possible Gas Mark. Cut your chosen fruit into thin slices, spread out on a large baking sheet, then place them in the oven for 12 hours, or until dried. Label and store in an airtight container in a cool, dry place for up to 1 month.

FRUIT JUICES

GRILLED PINK AND WHITE GRAPEFRUIT JUICE
- 2 pink grapefruits, halved
- 2 white grapefruits, halved

Preheat the grill (broiler). Peel the grapefruit. (Set aside the peel and use it to make Burnt Graperfruit Peel, see left). Grill (broil) the fruits, cut-sides up, for 5 minutes. Remove from the grill and squeeze the juice, then strain through a china-cap (chinois) sieve into a 700 ml (24 fl oz) sterilized bottle (see page 256). Label and store in the refrigerator for up to 3 days.

SOFT LIME JUICE
- 400 g (14 oz/ 1¾ cups) full-fat (whole) yogurt
- 300 ml (10 fl oz) fresh lime juice

Place the yogurt in a Thermomix® (see page 230 for alternative options) and set the temperature at 60°C (140°F) at minimum speed. Once the temperature is reached, switch off the heat, add the lime juice and blend at maximum speed for 10 seconds. Strain through a paper coffee filter into a 700 ml (24 fl oz) sterilized bottle (see page 256).

Label and store in the refrigerator for up to 3 days.

YUZU JUICE
- 600 ml (20 fl oz) fresh lemon juice
- 300 ml (10 fl oz) fresh yuzu juice

Combine the lemon and yuzu juices together in a large container, then pour into a 700 ml (24 fl oz) sterilized bottle (see page 256). Label and store in the refrigerator for up to 1 day.

GARNISHES

CRUNCHY BARLEY SPONGE
- 360 g (12 oz) egg whites
- 250 g (9 oz) egg yolks
- 22 g (¾ oz) baking powder
- 2 g (¼ teaspoon) sea salt
- 5 teaspoons barley coffee powder
- 60 g (2 oz) plain (all-purpose) flour
- Black food colouring

Mix all the egg whites and egg yolks together, then mix in the baking powder, salt, barley coffee and flour until combined. Stir in enough black food colouring until you reach the colour you like. Load the mixture into a whipped cream dispenser to about half of a soda siphon and add one canister of NO2 every 2 minutes, shaking every time you charge a new one. (Alternatively, if you don't have a whipped cream dispenser, whip the ingredients with an electric whisk.) After the third canister, leave the mixture to rest in the refrigerator for about 2 hours. Preheat the oven to 50°C/122°F/ lowest possible Gas Mark. Fill paper cups with the mixture until they are half-full, then microwave for 30 seconds. Transfer the cups to a baking sheet and leave to dry out in the oven for 6 hours. Label and store in an airtight container in a cool, dry place for 1 week.

BLUE DISC WATER CAKES
- 300 ml (10 fl oz) still mineral water
- 100 ml (3½ fl oz) Sugar Syrup (page 245)
- 5 g (⅛ oz) agar agar powder
- Blue food colouring
- 1 drop bergamot food-grade essential oil

Add all the ingredients to a Thermomix® (see page 230 for alternative options) and set it on VAROMA temperature (120°C/250°F).

Once it has reached the temperature, pour 15 ml (1 tablespoon) of the liquid into a disc stamp or silicone disc cake mould, 10 cm/4 inches in diameter and 2.3 cm/1 inch deep. This recipe makes enough for about 12 disc cakes. Leave them to cool and set in the refrigerator. Once they are solid, remove and transfer to a large airtight container. Label and store in the refrigerator for up to 1 week.

PEACH SPHERE WATER CAKES

- 600 ml (20 fl oz) Clarified White Peach Purée (page 233)
- 100 ml (3½ fl oz) Sugar Syrup (page 245)
- 10 g (¼ oz) agar agar powder
- 2 drops elicrisio food-grade essential oil

Place all the ingredients in a Thermomix® (see page 230 for alternative options) and set it on VAROMA temperature (120°C/250°F). Once it has reached the required temperature, pour it into the sphere stamps or silicone ice ball moulds, 5 cm/2 inches in diameter. This recipe makes enough for about 20 spheres. Leave to cool in the refrigerator for 30 minutes, or until solid. Once the spheres are solid, pierce the spheres with metal sticks or skewers. Store in an airtight container in the refrigerator for up to 3 days.

RED LIME DISC WATER CAKES

- 300 ml (10 fl oz) still mineral water
- 100 ml (3½ fl oz) Sugar Syrup (page 245)
- 5 g (⅛ oz) agar agar powder
- Red food colouring
- 1 drop lime food-grade essential oil

Place all the ingredients in a Thermomix® (see page 230 for alternative options) and set it on VAROMA temperature (120°C/250°F). Once it has reached the temperature, pour 15 ml (1 tablespoon) of the liquid into a disc stamp or silicone disc cake mould, 10 cm/4 inches in diameter and 2.3 cm/1 inch deep. This recipe makes enough for about 12 disc cakes. Leave in the refrigerator for 30 minutes, or until cool and set, then transfer to a large airtight container. Label and store in the refrigerator for up to 1 week.

RED SALTY LIME DISC WATER CAKES

- 300 ml (10 fl oz) still mineral water
- 100 ml (3½ fl oz) Sugar Syrup (page 245)
- 5 g (⅛ oz) agar agar powder
- Red food colouring
- 1 drop lime food-grade essential oil
- 5 g (⅛ oz) Maldon sea salt

Place all the ingredients in a Thermomix® (see page 230 for alternative options) and set it on VAROMA temperature (120°C/250°F). Once it has reached the temperature, pour 15 ml (1 tablespoon) of the liquid into a disc stamp or silicone disc cake mould, 10 cm/4 inches in diameter and 2.3 cm/1 inch deep. This recipe makes enough for about 12 disc cakes. Leave in the refrigerator for 30 minutes, or until cool and set, then transfer to a large airtight container. Label and store in the refrigerator for up to 1 week.

BLACK ISOMALT DISCS STUDDED WITH SESAME SEEDS

- 500 g (1 lb 2 oz) isomalt
- 2 drops black food colouring
- Sesame seeds, to sprinkle

Heat the isomalt in a large, nonstick saucepan over a medium heat for 4 minutes, or until it has turned into a liquid. Add the black food colouring. Pour big drops of the coloured isomalt onto a nonstick baking tray and sprinkle sesame seeds on top. Leave to set until solid. Label and store in an airtight container in a cool, dry place for up to 2 weeks.

CLEAR ISOMALT DISCS

- 500 g (1 lb 2 oz) isomalt

Heat the isomalt in a large, nonstick saucepan over a medium heat for 4 minutes, or until it has turned into a liquid. Pour big drops of the isomalt onto a nonstick baking tray and leave to set. Store in an airtight container in a cool, dry place for up to 2 weeks.

CLEAR ISOMALT DISCS STUDDED WITH POLLEN

- 500 g (1 lb 2 oz) isomalt
- Bee pollen, to sprinkle

Heat the isomalt in a large, nonstick saucepan over a medium heat for 4 minutes, or until it has turned into a liquid. Pour big drops of the isomalt onto a nonstick baking tray and sprinkle the bee pollen on top. Leave to set, then label and store in an airtight container at room temperature for up to 2 weeks.

CLEAR ISOMALT SPIKES

- 500 g (1 lb 2 oz) isomalt

Heat the isomalt in a large nonstick saucepan over a medium heat for 4 minutes, or until it has turned into a liquid. Spread a thin layer on a nonstick baking tray and leave to dry. Once dried, break the isomalt up creating spikes. Transfer to an airtight container and add strips of foil between each spike so they aren't touching. Label and store in a cool, dry place for up to 2 weeks.

MANGO AND GREEN MANDARIN LEATHER LEAVES

- 350 ml (12 fl oz) fresh mango purée
- 150 g (5 fl oz/ ⅔ cup) still mineral water
- 75 g (2 ¾ oz) pectin
- 75 g (2 ¾ oz/ ⅓ cup) caster (superfine) sugar
- 1 drop mandarino verde food-grade essential oil

Preheat the oven to 50°C/122°F/ lowest possible Gas Mark. Place all the ingredients, except the essential oil, in a Thermomix® (see page 230 for alternative options) and set it at VAROMA temperature (120°C/250°F) and minimum speed. Once it reaches the temperature, add the essential oil and quickly blend it. Pour the mixture into a silicone tropical leaf mould and spread it out so all the leaves are filled. Transfer to the oven for 40 minutes, then remove the leaves and place in an airtight container. Label and store in a cool, dry place for up to 1 week.

INFUSIONS

COCOA BEAN-INFUSED AMARO LUCANO

- 700 ml (24 fl oz) Amaro Lucano
- 150 g (5 oz) cocoa beans

Combine the amaro and cocoa beans in a large container and leave to infuse for 24 hours. Strain through a paper coffee filter into a 700 ml (24 fl oz) sterilized bottle (see page 256). Label and store at room temperature for up to 1 month.

BEE POLLEN-INFUSED ARMAGNAC

- 700 ml (24 fl oz) Armagnac
- 50 g (2 oz) bee pollen

Stir the Armagnac and bee pollen together in a jug, then strain through a paper coffee filter into a 700 ml (24 fl oz) sterilized bottle (see page 256). Label and store at room temperature for up to 1 month.

FRESH CARDAMOM LEAF-INFUSED BOURBON

- 4 dried cardamom leaves
- 700 ml (24 fl oz) bourbon

Place the cardamom leaves in the bourbon bottle or combine the leaves and bourbon in a large container and leave to infuse for 24 hours. Strain through a paper coffee filter into a 700 ml (24 fl oz) sterilized bottle (see page 256). Label and store at room temperature for up to 1 month.

COCONUT AND COFFEE-INFUSED CACHAÇA

- 700 ml (24 fl oz) cachaça
- 150 g (5 oz) coconut flakes
- 10 g (¼ oz) ground coffee

Gently blend the cachaça and coconut flakes in a blender, then leave to infuse for 3 hours. Pour the ground coffee into the base of a paper coffee filter, then strain the cachaça mixture through the filter into a large freezerproof container. Freeze for 24 hours. Strain through a paper coffee filter into a 700 ml (24 fl oz) sterilized bottle (see page 256). Label and store in the refrigerator for up to 1 month.

ORANGE, CLEMENTINE AND SZECHUAN PEPPER-INFUSED COCCHI AMERICANO

- 150 g (5 oz/ ¾ cup) caster (superfine) sugar
- 30 g (1 oz) clementine peels
- 1 litre (34 fl oz) Cocchi Americano (quinine-flavoured apéritif wine)
- 30 g (1 oz) dried orange peels
- 3 g (½ teaspoon) Szechuan peppercorns
- 30 ml (1 fl oz) orange blossom water

Place the sugar and clementine peels in a sous-vide vacuum bag (or plastic resealable bag) and seal. Place the Cocchi Americano, dried orange peels and peppercorns in a separate sous-vide bag and seal. Cook both bags in a sous-vide bath (see page 230 for alternative options) at 65°C (149°F) for 1 hour. Pour the contents of both bags into a large container and stir until the sugar has completely dissolved. Add the orange blossom water. Strain into a 700 ml (24 fl oz) sterilized bottle (see page 256). Label and store in the refrigerator for up to 1 month.

MACE-INFUSED COCCHI ROSA

- 10 g (¼ oz) mace
- 600 ml (20 fl oz) Cocchi Rosa (rosè quinine flavoured aperitif)

Place the mace in the Cocchi Rosa bottle or combine the mace and Cocchi Rosa in a large container and leave to infuse for 24 hours. Strain through a paper coffee filter into a 700 ml (24 fl oz) sterilized bottle (see page 256). Label and store in the refrigerator for up to 1 month.

DANDELION COFFEE-INFUSED COGNAC

- 15 g (½ oz) dandelion root coffee
- 750 ml (25 fl oz) cognac

Place the dandelion root coffee in the cognac bottle or combine the dandelion root coffee and cognac in a large container and leave to steep for 2 hours. Strain through a paper coffee filter into a 700 ml (24 fl oz) sterilized bottle (see page 256). Label and store at room temperature for up to 1 month.

CACAO NIB-INFUSED GENEVER

- 20 g (¾ oz) cacao nibs
- 700 ml (24 fl oz) genever

Place the cacao nibs in the genever bottle or combine the cacao nibs and genever in a large container and leave to infuse for 24 hours. Strain through a paper coffee filter into a 700 ml (24 fl oz) sterilized bottle (see page 256). Label and store at room temperature for up to 1 month.

MAKRUT LIME LEAF-INFUSED GENEVER

- 10 makrut lime leaves
- 700 ml (24 fl oz) genever

Place the leaves in the genever bottle or combine the leaves and genever in a large container and leave to infuse for 24 hours. Strain through a paper coffee filter into a 700 ml (24 fl oz) sterilized bottle (see page 256). Label and store at room temperature for up to 1 month.

PINE-INFUSED GIN

- 20 fresh pine needles
- 700 ml (24 fl oz) celery gin

Place the pine needles in the gin bottle or combine the pine needles and gin in a large container and leave to infuse for 24 hours. Fine strain through a muslin cloth (cheesecloth) into a 700 ml (24 fl oz) sterilized bottle (see page 256). Label and store at room temperature for up to 1 month.

TOMATO SKIN-INFUSED JAPANESE GIN

- 750 ml (25 fl oz) Japanese gin
- 30 cherry tomatoes, halved

Combine the gin and the tomatoes in a large jug (pitcher) and leave to infuse for 2 days. Strain through a paper coffee filter into a 700 ml (24 fl oz) sterilized bottle (see page 256). Label and store in the refrigerator for up to 1 month.

TAMARILLO AND TEA-INFUSED KOMBUCHA

- 1 litre (34 fl oz) kombucha
- 6 tamarillos, roughly chopped
- 15 ml (½ fl oz) brewed jasmine tea

Muddle the kombucha, tamarillos and tea in a large jug (pitcher) and leave to infuse for 2 hours. Fine strain through a muslin cloth (cheesecloth) into a 700 ml (24 fl oz) sterilized bottle (see page 256). Label and store in the refrigerator for up to 3 days.

SAFFRON-INFUSED LILLET BLANC

- 1 g (2 barspoons) saffron threads
- 750 ml (25 fl oz) Lillet Blanc

Place the saffron in the Lillet Blanc bottle or combine the saffron and Lillet Blanc in a large container and leave to infuse for 2 hours. Strain through a paper coffee filter into a 700 ml (24 fl oz) sterilized bottle (see page 256). Label and store in the refrigerator for up to 1 month.

KORERIMA POD-INFUSED MASTIHA

- 700 ml (24 fl oz) mastiha (Greek liquor made with a local resin)
- 105 g (3½ oz) Korerima pods (grains of paradise)

Combine the mastiha and Korerima pods in a large jug (pitcher) and leave to infuse for 24 hours. Strain through a paper coffee filter into a 700 ml (24 fl oz) sterilized bottle (see page 256). Label and store at room temperature for up to 1 month.

APRICOT KERNEL-INFUSED PISCO

- 750 ml (25 fl oz) pisco
- 20 g (¾ oz) apricot kernels (pits)

Combine the pisco and apricot kernels (pits) in a large jug (pitcher) and leave to infuse for 24 hours. Strain through a paper coffee filter into a 700 ml (24 fl oz) sterilized bottle (see page 256). Label and store at room temperature for up to 1 month.

WILD CHERRY BARK-INFUSED PISCO

- 15 g (½ oz) wild cherry bark
- 750 ml (25 fl oz) pisco

Place the wild cherry bark in the pisco bottle or combine the wild cherry bark and pisco in a large container and leave to infuse for 3 hours. Fine strain through a muslin cloth (cheesecloth) into a 700 ml (24 fl oz) sterilized bottle (see page 256). Label and store at room temperature for up to 1 month.

WATTLESEED-INFUSED VENEZUELAN-STYLE RUM

- 500 ml (17 fl oz) Venezuelan rum
- 250 ml (8 fl oz) rye whiskey
- 10 g (¼ oz) wattleseeds

Place the rum, whiskey and wattleseeds in a sous-vide vacuum bag (or plastic resealable bag) and seal. Place the bag in an ultrasound machine (see page 230 for alternative options) and leave to infuse to for 30 minutes. Strain through a paper coffee filter into a 700 ml (24 fl oz) sterilized bottle (see page 256). Label and store at room temperature for up to 1 month.

WATTLESEED-INFUSED RYE

- 700 ml (24 fl oz) rye whiskey
- 10 g (¼ oz) wattleseeds

Place the whiskey and wattleseeds in a sous-vide vacuum bag (or plastic resealable bag) and seal. Place the bag in an ultrasound machine (see page 230 for alternative options) and leave to infuse for 30 minutes. Strain through a paper coffee filter into a 700 ml (24 fl oz) sterilized bottle (see page 256). Label and store at room temperature for up to 1 month.

ROASTED PINEAPPLE-INFUSED AGED BLENDED SCOTCH

- 250 g (9 oz) fresh pineapple slices, skin on
- 700 ml (24 fl oz) aged, blended Scotch whisky

Preheat the grill (broiler). Roast the pineapple slices under the grill until evenly cooked. Chop the grilled pineapple, transfer it to a large jug (pitcher), add the whisky and leave to infuse for 24 hours. Strain through a paper coffee filter into a 700 ml (24 fl oz) sterilized bottle (see page 256). Label and store in the refrigerator for up to 1 month.

SARSAPARILLA-INFUSED SODA WATER

- 50 ml (1¾ fl oz) sarsaparilla cordial
- 700 ml (24 fl oz) still mineral water

Pour the cordial and water into a soda siphon. Charge with 2 CO_2 chargers and refrigerate. You can store the soda water without charging it in a 700 ml (24 fl oz) sterilized bottle (see page 256) in the refrigerator for up to 1 month.

AMALFI LEMON PEEL-INFUSED VERMOUTH

- 4 Amalfi lemons peels
- 700 ml (24 fl oz) Martini Riserva Speciale Ambrato

Place the lemon peels and Ambrato in a sous-vide vacuum bag (or plastic resealable bag) and seal. Cook in a sous-vide bath (see page 230 for alternative options) at 45°C (113°F) for 90 minutes. Strain through a paper coffee filter into a 700 ml (24 fl oz) sterilized bottle (see page 256). Label and store in the refrigerator for up to 1 month.

BLACKBERRY-INFUSED SWEET VERMOUTH

- 200 g (7 oz) fresh blackberries

- 1 litre (34 fl oz) sweet vermouth

Mix the blackberries and vermouth together in a blender, then leave to infuse for 1 hour. Strain through a paper coffee filter into a 700 ml (24 fl oz) sterilized bottle (see page 256). Label and store in the refrigerator for up to 1 month.

COFFEE BEAN-INFUSED EXTRA DRY VERMOUTH

- 750 ml (25 fl oz) Martini Extra Dry
- 30 g (1 oz) coffee beans

Combine the Martini Extra Dry and coffee beans in a large jug (pitcher) and leave to infuse for 24 hours. Strain through a paper coffee filter into a 700 ml (24 fl oz) sterilized bottle (see page 256). Label and store in the refrigerator for up to 1 month.

WATTLESEED-INFUSED VERMOUTH

- 700 ml (24 fl oz) Martini Riserva Speciale Ambrato
- 10 g (¼ oz) wattleseeds
- 10 g (¼ oz) cacao nibs

Combine the Ambrato, wattleseeds and cacao nibs in a large container and leave to infuse for 2 hours. Fine strain through a muslin cloth (cheesecloth) into a 700 ml (24 fl oz) sterilized bottle (see page 256). Label and store in the refrigerator for up to 1 month.

BARBERRY AND MULBERRY-INFUSED VODKA

- 700 ml (24 fl oz) vodka
- 25 g (1 oz) barberries
- 5 g (⅛ oz) sweet mulberries

Place the vodka, barberries and mulberries in a sous-vide vacuum bag (or plastic resealable bag) and seal. Place the bag in an ultrasound machine (see page 230 for alternative options) and leave to infuse for 30 minutes. Strain through a paper coffee filter into a 700 ml (24 fl oz) sterilized bottle (see page 256). Label and store at room temperature for up to 1 month.

COCOA BEAN-INFUSED VODKA

- 700 ml (24 fl oz) multi-grain vodka
- 25 g (1 oz) cocoa beans

Combine the vodka and cocoa beans in a large container and leave to infuse for 24 hours.

Fine strain through a muslin cloth (cheesecloth) into a 700 ml (24 fl oz) sterilized bottle (see page 256). Label and store in the refrigerator for up to 1 month.

PASSION FRUIT SEED-INFUSED VODKA

- 20 g (¾ oz) passion fruit seeds
- 700 ml (24 fl oz) vodka

Place the passion fruit seeds in the vodka bottle or combine the passion fruit seeds and vodka in a large container and leave to infuse for 24 hours. Fine strain through a muslin cloth (cheesecloth) into a 700 ml (24 fl oz) sterilized bottle (see page 256). Label and store at room temperature for up to 1 month.

EARL GREY TEA-INFUSED PORT WINE

- 10 g (¼ oz) Earl Grey tea leaves
- 750 ml (25 fl oz) port wine

Place the tea in the bottle of port or combine the tea and port in a large container and leave to infuse for 4 hours. Strain through a paper coffee filter into a 700 ml (24 fl oz) sterilized bottle (see page 256). Label and store in the refrigerator for up to 1 month.

SPICE-INFUSED SANCERRE WINE

- 625 ml (21 fl oz) Sancerre wine
- 250 g (9 oz) piece of fresh root ginger, peeled and chopped
- 375 ml (12¾ fl oz) fino sherry
- 5 cardamom leaves
- 15 g (½ oz) Vietnamese pepper berries
- 100 g (3½ oz/ ½ cup) caster (superfine) sugar

Place the Sancerre and ginger in a sous-vide vacuum bag (or plastic resealable bag) and seal. Place the sherry, cardamom leaves and pepper berries in a separate sous-vide bag and seal. Cook both bags in a sous-vide bath (see page 230 for alternative options) at 60°C (140°F) for 1 hour. Strain through a paper coffee filter and blend the contents of both bags together in a large jug (pitcher). Add the sugar and stir until dissolved. Pour into a 700 ml (24 fl oz) sterilized bottle (see page 256). Label and store in the refrigerator for up to 1 week.

LIQUEUR

OAT LIQUEUR

- 600 ml (20 fl oz) Japanese vodka
- 70 g (2¾ oz/ ¾ cup) rolled oats
- 100 ml (3½ fl oz) Sugar Syrup (page 245)

Place the vodka and oats in a sous-vide vacuum bag (or plastic resealable bag) and seal. Place the bag in an ultrasound machine (see page 230 for alternative options) with no temperature for 30 minutes. Strain the mixture through a paper coffee filter into a large jug (pitcher), add the sugar syrup and stir to combine. Pour into a 700 ml (24 fl oz) sterilized bottle (see page 256). Label and store at room temperature for up to 1 month.

MILKS AND CREAM

COCOA HUSK CREAM

- 100 g (3½ oz/ ½ cup) caster (superfine) sugar
- 30 ml (1 fl oz) fresh lemon juice
- 300 ml (10 fl oz) single (light) cream
- 30 ml (1 fl oz) Galliano L'Autentico
- ½ whole nutmeg, grated
- 15 g (½ oz) cocoa husks (cacao shells)
- 15 g (½ oz) cacao nibs

Place the sugar, lemon juice, cream, Galliano L'Autentico, nutmeg, cocoa husks (cacao shells) and cacao nibs in a blender and mix. Transfer to a 700 ml (24 fl oz) sterilized bottle (see page 256), label and store in the refrigerator for up to 2 days.

PASSION FRUIT AND PASSION BERRY MILK

- 350 ml (12 fl oz) reposado tequila
- 175 ml (6 fl oz) Martini Riserva Speciale Ambrato
- 200 ml (7 fl oz) brewed milk oolong tea
- 40 g (1½ oz) Ethiopian passion berries
- 400 g (14 oz/1 ¾ cups) double (heavy) cream
- 200 ml (7 fl oz) passion fruit purée
- 20 g (¾ fl oz) fresh lemon juice

Place the tequila, Ambrato, tea and berries in a sous-vide vacuum bag (or plastic resealable bag) and seal. Place the bag in an ultrasound machine (see page 230 for alternative options) and leave to infuse for 30 minutes. Pour the contents into a large container and add the cream, purée and lemon juice. Leave to stand for 30 minutes, or until curdled. Strain through a paper coffee filter into a 700 ml (24 fl oz) sterilized bottle (see page 256). Label and store in the refrigerator for up to 3 days.

PISTACHIO AND RASPBERRY MILK

- 600 ml (20 fl oz) bourbon
- 200 ml (7 fl oz) brewed black tea
- 200 g (7 oz/1 cup) caster (superfine) sugar
- 40 ml (1⅓ fl oz) fresh lemon juice
- 260 g (9¼ oz) raspberry purée
- 40 g (1½ oz) pistachio cream
- 500 ml (17 fl oz) full-fat (whole) milk

Combine the bourbon, tea, sugar and lemon juice in a container and set aside. Place the purée, cream and milk in a Thermomix® (see page 230 for alternative options) and blitz at full speed for 10 seconds. Add the bourbon mixture and cook at 60°C (140°F) until curdled. Strain through a paper coffee filter into a 700 ml (24 fl oz) sterilized bottle (see page 256). Label and store in the refrigerator for up to 2 days.

TROPICAL MILK JAM

- 200 ml (7 fl oz) Connaught Bar Sweet Vermouth Mix (page 241)
- 100 ml (3½ fl oz) Bitters Mix (page 241)
- 200 ml (7 fl oz) aged rum
- 150 ml (5 fl oz) sherry
- 150 ml (5 fl oz) full-fat (whole) milk
- 150 ml (5 fl oz) liqueur de noix
- 150 ml (5 fl oz) mango purée
- 100 g (3½ oz/ ½ cup) caster (superfine) sugar

Place the vermouth, bitters, rum and sherry in a large jug (pitcher), then stir until mixed and set aside. Place the milk, liqueur, purée, and sugar in a Thermomix® (see page 230 for alternative options) and cook at 60°C (140°F) for 10 minutes at minimum speed. Pour into a separate jug, then pour the milk mixture into the vermouth mixture and leave to rest for at least 30 minutes, or until it curdles. Strain through a paper coffee filter into a 700 ml (24 fl oz) sterilized bottle (see page 256). Label and store in the refrigerator for up to 1 week.

COFFEE AND PINEAPPLE MILK PUNCH

- 200 ml (7 fl oz) cognac
- 100 ml (3½ fl oz) aged Jamaican rum
- 175 ml (6 fl oz) cold-pressed pineapple juice
- 25 g (1 oz/scant 1 tablespoon) caster (superfine) sugar
- 25 ml (¾ fl oz) brewed espresso
- 300 ml (10 fl oz) full-fat (whole) milk

Place the cognac, rum, pineapple juice, sugar and espresso in a large container and mix well. Add the milk and stir to combine. When the liquid curdles, strain through a paper coffee filter into a 700 ml (24 fl oz) sterilized bottle (see page 256). Label and store in the refrigerator for up to 1 week.

COPPER AND BLUE MILK PUNCH

For the Copper and Blue mix
- 480 ml (16 fl oz) Martini Riserva Speciale Ambrato
- 120 ml (4 fl oz) Bacardi
- 120 ml (4 fl oz) Plantation Pineapple Rum
- 120 ml (4 fl oz) pineapple juice
- 4 passion fruit seeds

For the milk and cream
- 150 ml (5 fl oz) whole milk
- 150 ml (5 fl oz) coconut cream
- 30 ml (1 fl oz) fresh lemon juice

To make the Copper and Blue mix, combine all the ingredients together in a large container. To make the milk and cream, heat the milk and coconut cream in a large saucepan over a low heat until it reaches 60°C (140°F) on a thermometer. Pour the milk and cream mixture into the Copper and Blue mix with the lemon juice and leave to rest for 45 minutes. Strain through a paper coffee filter into a 700 ml (24 fl oz) sterilized bottle (see page 256). Label and store in the refrigerator for up to 1 week.

ELLIPSIS MILK PUNCH

For the milk jam
- 1 litre (34 fl oz) full-fat (whole) milk
- 15 ml (½ fl oz) vanilla extract
- 300 g (11 oz/1 ½ cups) caster (superfine) sugar

For the mix
- 300 ml (10 fl oz) Armagnac
- 200 ml (7 fl oz) fino sherry
- 150 ml (5 fl oz) blended rum
- 200 ml (7 fl oz) Martini Riserva Speciale Ambrato
- 200 ml (7 fl oz) Chablis wine
- 30 ml (1 fl oz) fresh lemon juice

To make the milk jam, place the milk, extract and sugar in the Thermomix® (see page 230 for alternative options). Cook at maximum heat for 10 minutes, or until it reduces by half and turns a caramel colour. Meanwhile, to make the mix, pour the armagnac, sherry, rum, Ambrato, wine and lemon juice into a large container. When the milk jam is ready, pour it into the spirit mixture and leave to rest until it curdles. Strain it through a paper coffee filter into a 700 ml (24 fl oz) sterilized bottle (see page 256). Label and store in the refrigerator for up to 1 week.

FLOAT LIKE A BUTTERFLY MILK PUNCH

- 250 g (9 oz/1 ¼ cups) caster (superfine) sugar
- 30 g (5 teaspoons) fennel seeds
- Grated zest of 3 lemons
- 200 g (7 oz) celery, chopped
- 750 g (1 lb 10 oz) pineapple with rind, chopped
- 160 ml (5½ fl oz) fresh lemon juice
- 300 ml (10 fl oz) brewed lemon verbena tea
- 350 ml (12 fl oz) bourbon
- 200 ml (7 fl oz) tequila
- 75 ml (2½ fl oz) absinthe
- 300 ml (10 fl oz) full-fat (whole) milk

Place the sugar, fennel seeds, lemon zest, celery and pineapple in a large jug (pitcher) and muddle well. Add 100 ml (3 ½ fl oz) of the lemon juice and the lemon verbena tea, bourbon, tequila and absinthe and leave to infuse for 24 hours. Fine strain through a muslin cloth (cheesecloth) into another jug. Heat the milk in a small saucepan for a few minutes until warm, but boiling. Slowly pour the hot milk and the remaining 60 ml (2 fl oz) of lemon juice into the jug and leave to infuse for 30 minutes. Fine strain the mixture through two pieces of muslin cloth into a clean jug and leave to infuse for another 5 hours, then gently pour into a 700 ml

(24 fl oz) sterilized bottle (see page 256), making sure you leave the sediment behind. Label and store in the refrigerator for up to 1 week.

MAGNETUM MILK PUNCH

- 250 g (9 oz/1 ¼ cups) caster (superfine) sugar
- 25 g (1 oz) fennel seeds
- 750 g (26½ oz) pineapple, chopped with rind
- 200 g (7 oz) fennel bulb, chopped
- Grated zest of 3 lemons
- 160 ml (5½ fl oz) fresh lemon juice
- 300 ml (10 fl oz) brewed lemon verbena tea
- 550 ml (18 fl oz) fino sherry
- 75 ml (2½ fl oz) Galliano L'Autentico
- 300 ml (10 fl oz) full-fat (whole) milk

In a large jug (pitcher) or wide-mouthed jar, add the sugar, fennel seeds, pineapple, fennel bulb and lemon zest and muddle until all the ingredients are crushed. Add the lemon juice, lemon verbena tea, sherry and Galliano L'Autentico. Cover with a lid and leave to infuse for 24 hours. The next day, heat the milk in a Thermomix® (see page 230 for alternative options) until it reaches 60°C (140°F). Meanwhile, fine strain the infused mixture through a muslin cloth (cheesecloth) into another large heatproof container and add the heated milk. Leave to infuse for 30 minutes, or until the mixture curdles. Strain through a paper coffee filter into a 700 ml (24 fl oz) sterilized bottle (see page 256). Label and store in the refrigerator for up to 1 week.

PRIMO COCONUT MILK PUNCH

For the Primo mix
- 300 ml (10 fl oz) aged Cuban rum
- 100 ml (3½ fl oz) Muyu Chinotto Nero Liqueur
- 300 ml (10 fl oz) Martini Riserva Speciale Rubino
- 50 ml (1¾ fl oz) Italian espresso liqueur
- 100 ml (3½ fl oz) Amaro Lucano

For the milk and cream
- 150 ml (5 fl oz) coconut cream
- 150 ml (5 fl oz) full-fat (whole) milk
- 10 g (¼ oz) cocoa powder
- 10 g (¼ oz) dill seeds
- Grated zest of 1 orange
- 30 ml (1 fl oz) fresh lemon juice

To make the Primo mix, combine all the ingredients together in a large container. Set aside.

To make the milk and cream, heat the coconut cream and milk in a large saucepan over a low heat until it reaches 60°C (140°F) on a thermometer, then add the cocoa powder, dill seeds and orange zest. Pour the milk and cream mixture into the Primo mix with the lemon juice and leave to rest for 30 minutes. Strain through a coffee filter paper into a 700 ml (24 fl oz) sterilized bottle (see page 256). Label and store in the refrigerator for up to 1 week.

SWEET AND Z MILK PUNCH

For the Negroni
- 600 ml (20 fl oz) reposado tequila
- 600 ml (20 fl oz) Connaught Bar Sweet Vermouth Mix (page 241)
- 600 ml (20 fl oz) Galliano l'Aperitivo

For the cream
- 300 ml (10 fl oz) single (light) cream
- ½ whole nutmeg, grated
- 15 g (½ oz) cocoa husks (cacao shells)
- 15 g (½ oz) cacoa nibs
- 100 g (3½ oz) caster (superfine) sugar
- 30 ml (1 fl oz) Galliano l'Autentico
- 30 ml (1 fl oz) fresh lemon juice

To make the Negroni, place the tequila, vermouth and Galliano l'Aperitivo in a large heatproof container. Set aside. To make the cream, heat the cream, nutmeg, cocoa husks (cacao shells), cacao nibs and sugar in a large saucepan over a low heat until it reaches 60°C (140°F) on a thermometer. Add the cream and Galliano l'Autentico, then slowly pour in the lemon juice. Pour into the container and leave to infuse for 45 minutes. Strain through a paper coffee filter into a 700 ml (24 fl oz) sterilized bottle (see page 256). Label and store in the refrigerator for up to 1 week.

MIXES AND PRE-MIXES

BITTERS MIX
- 350 ml (12 fl oz) Campari
- 350 ml (12 fl oz) Galliano l'Aperitivo

Combine the ingredients in a jug (pitcher). Strain through a paper coffee filter into a 700 ml (24 fl oz) sterilized bottle (see page 256). Label and store at room temperature for up to 1 month.

BLOODY MARY MIX
- 20 coriander (cilantro) sprigs
- 10 g (¼ oz) English mustard
- 30 drops Tabasco sauce
- 5 cm (2 inch) piece fresh horseradish, grated
- 30 ml (1 fl oz) soy sauce
- 600 ml (20 fl oz) Worcestershire sauce
- Pinch of sea salt
- Small slice of Naga Jolokia chilli (ghost chilli) or other fresh red chilli of choice

Place all the ingredients in a blender and mix for a few seconds. Strain through a paper coffee filter into a 700 ml (24 fl oz) sterilized bottle (see page 256). Label and store in the refrigerator for up to 1 week.

CONNAUGHT BAR DRY VERMOUTH MIX
- 250 ml (8 fl oz) Noilly Prat
- 250 ml (8 fl oz) Martini Extra Dry
- 250 ml (8 fl oz) Gancia Bianco

Combine all three vermouths together in a large container, then pour into a 700 ml (24 fl oz) sterilized bottle (see page 256). Label and store in the refrigerator for up to 2 weeks.

CONNAUGHT BAR SWEET VERMOUTH MIX
- 250 ml (8 fl oz) Martini Rosso
- 250 ml (8 fl oz) Punt e Mes
- 250 ml (8 fl oz) 1757 vermouth di Torino

Combine all three vermouths in a 700 ml (24 fl oz) sterilized bottle (see page 256) and shake lightly to combine. Label and store in the refrigerator for up to 2 weeks.

ECLIPSE PRE-MIX
- 800 ml (28 fl oz) Connaught Bar Sweet Vermouth Mix (see above)
- 400 ml (14 fl oz) Bitters Mix (see left)
- 60 ml (2 fl oz) fresh lemon juice
- 2 drops bergamot food-grade essential oil
- 700 g (1 lb 8½ oz/ generous 3 cups) cream cheese
- 400 g (14 oz) caster (superfine) sugar

- 10 g (¼ oz) cocoa husks (cacao shells)
- 10 g (¼ oz) cocoa powder
- 60 g (2 fl oz) Savoia Americano Rosso Amaro Dolce

Combine the vermouth, bitters mix and lemon juice in the Thermomix® (see page 230 for alternative options). Blend at full speed for a few seconds, then set to low speed to bring it to 80°C (176°F). Once it reaches temperature, pour the contents into a large container. Stir in the bergamot oil, cream cheese, sugar, cocoa husks (cacao shells), cocoa powder and Savoia Americano Rosso Amaro Dolce and leave to infuse for 30 minutes, or until curdled. Strain through a paper coffee filter into a 700 ml (24 fl oz) sterilized bottle (see page 256). Label and store in the refrigerator for up to 1 week.

MAGNETUM SHERRY-WHISKY MIX
- 600 ml (20 fl oz) single malt whisky
- 100 ml (3½ fl oz) Pedro Ximenez sherry

Pour the whisky and sherry into a 700 ml (24 fl oz) sterilized bottle (see page 256) or large container and mix together. Label and store in the refrigerator for up to 1 month.

MEMENTO MIX
- 200 ml (7 fl oz) cucumber and rose gin
- 200 ml (7 fl oz) Martini Riserva Speciale Ambrato
- 100 ml (3½ fl oz) genever
- 100 ml (3½ fl oz) sherry
- 20 × 20 cm (8 × 8 inch) square piece of marble, washed well
- 2 drops cypress food-grade essential oil

Place the gin, Ambrato, genever, sherry and piece of marble in a sous-vide vacuum bag (or plastic resealable bag) and seal. Cook in a sous-vide bath (see page 230 for alternative options) at 60°C (140°F) for 2 hours. When done, pour the mixture into a large container and add the cypress oil. Leave to cool. Strain through a paper coffee filter into a 700 ml (24 fl oz) sterilized bottle (see page 256). Label and store at room temperature for up to 1 month. Wash the piece of marble and reuse the next time you make the mix.

SET IN STONE MIX

- 300 ml (10 fl oz) gin
- 300 ml (10 fl oz) genever
- 200 ml (7 fl oz) Amontillado sherry
- 10 ml (2 teaspoons) tonka bitters (see page 256)
- 10 ml (2 teaspoons) Italicus Rosolio di Bergamotto
- 50 ml (1¾ fl oz) Sugar Syrup (page 245)
- 2 drops elicriso food-grade essential oil
- 10 × 10 × 5 cm (4 × 4 × 2 inch) piece of marble stone, washed well

Mix all the ingredients, except the piece of marble stone, together, then pour into a sous-vide vacuum bag (or plastic resealable bag), add the marble and seal. Cook in a sous-vide bath (see page 230 for alternative options) for 1 hour at 60°C (140°F). Remove the marble and pour into a 700 ml (24 fl oz) sterilized bottle (see page 256). Label and store in the refrigerator for up to 1 month. Wash the piece of marble and reuse the next time you make this mix.

POWDERS

COPPER-HUED POWDER

- 5 g (1 teaspoon) edible copper food powder
- 500 g (1 lb 2 oz/scant 4¼ cups) caster (superfine) sugar

In a bowl, mix together the copper food powder and sugar. Label and store in an airtight container in a cool, dry place for 1 month.

WATERMELON RIND AND JALAPEÑO POWDER

- 400 g (14 oz) watermelon rind
- 100 g (3½ oz) jalapeño chillies

Preheat the oven to 50°C/122°F/ lowest possible Gas Mark. Peel the watermelon rind, trying to get as little pith on the rinds as possible, then spread them out on a large baking sheet together with the chillies. Place them in the oven for 12 hours, or until dried. Once dried transfer the peel and chillies to a blender and blitz until ground. Label and store in an airtight container at room temperature for up to 1 month.

SHERBETS

ALMOND SHERBET

- 375 ml (13 fl oz) fresh lemon juice
- 125 g (4½ oz/scant ⅔ cup) caster (superfine) sugar
- 5 ml (1 barspoon) vanilla extract
- 75 ml (2½ fl oz) orgeat
- 300 ml (10 fl oz) still mineral water
- Peel of 6 lemons

Place the lemon juice, sugar, extract, orgeat, mineral water and lemon peels into the Thermomix® (see page 230 for alternative options) and cook at 40°C (104°F) for 30 minutes. When done, strain through a paper coffee filter into a 700 ml (24 fl oz) sterilized bottle (see page 256). Label and store in the refrigerator for up to 1 week.

BERGAMOT AND BASIL SHERBET

- 800 g (1¾ lb/4 cups) caster (superfine) sugar
- 20 g (¾ oz) fennel seeds
- 10 basil leaves
- 1 litre (34 fl oz) bergamot juice

Place the sugar, fennel seeds and basil leaves in a large container. Gently muddle and stir to combine the ingredients. Add the bergamot juice and leave to infuse for 1 hour, stirring occasionally until the sugar is dissolved. Strain through a paper coffee filter into a 700 ml (24 fl oz) sterilized bottle (see page 256). Label and store in the refrigerator for up to 3 days.

GRILLED GRAPEFRUIT SHERBET

- 400 g (14 oz/2 cups) caster (superfine) sugar
- Burnt Grapefruit Peel (page 235)
- 1 litre (34 fl oz) Grilled Pink and White Grapefruit Juice (page 235)

Place the sugar and grapefruit peel in a large container, stir to mix and leave to rest for 30 minutes. Add the juice and stir until the sugar has completely dissolved. Fine strain through a muslin cloth (cheesecloth) into a 700 ml (24 fl oz) sterilized bottle (see page 256). Label and store in the refrigerator for up to 3 days.

LIME SHERBET

- Peels from 12 limes
- 200 g (7 oz/1 cup) caster (superfine) sugar

- 600 ml (20 fl oz) fresh lime juice

Place the lime peels and sugar in a large container and muddle the mixture to release the oils. Add the lime juice and leave to infuse for 30 minutes. Pour into a 700 ml (24 fl oz) sterilized bottle (see page 256), label and store in the refrigerator for up to 3 days.

PASSION FRUIT AND MAKRUT LIME SHERBET

- 10 g (¼ oz) fresh passion fruit pulp
- 500 g (1 lb 2 oz/2 ½ cups) caster (superfine) sugar
- Grated zest of 1 orange
- 10 makrut lime leaves
- 500 ml (17 fl oz) passion fruit purée

Combine the passion fruit pulp, sugar, orange zest and lime leaves in a large container and leave to infuse for 45 minutes. Add the purée and stir until the sugar dissolves. Strain through a paper coffee filter into a 700 ml (24 fl oz) sterilized bottle (see page 256). Label and store in the refrigerator for up to 1 week.

SEA BUCKTHORN SHERBET

- 350 ml (12 fl oz) sea buckthorn purée
- 350 g (12 oz/1 ¾ cups) caster (superfine) sugar
- 350 ml (12 fl oz) apple juice

Place the purée, sugar and apple juice in a large container and gently muddle to mix. Leave to infuse for 1 hour, stirring occasionally to dissolve the sugar. Strain through a paper coffee filter into a 700 ml (24 fl oz) sterilized bottle (see page 256). Label and store in the refrigerator for up to 1 week.

SPICY CALAMANSI SHERBET

- 1 litre (34 fl oz) calamansi purée
- 500 g (1 lb 2 oz/2 ½ cups) caster (superfine) sugar
- 15 g (½ oz) whole cloves
- 1 cinnamon stick
- ½ tonka bean (see page 256), grated

Place the purée, sugar, cloves, cinnamon stick and tonka bean in a blender to combine. Strain through a paper coffee filter into a 700 ml (24 fl oz) sterilized bottle (see page 256). Label and store in the refrigerator for up to 1 week.

SHRUBS

CLEMENTINE AND TONKA BEAN SHRUB

- 250 g (9 oz) clementine pulp
- 150 g (5 oz/¾ cup) caster (superfine) sugar
- 200 ml (7 fl oz) champagne vinegar
- ½ tonka bean (see page 256), grated
- 250 ml (8 fl oz) clementine juice

Add the pulp, sugar, vinegar and grated tonka bean to a Thermomix® (see page 230 for alternative options). Blend quickly, then set to cook at 60°C (140°F) for 30 minutes. Strain through a paper coffee filter into a large container and leave to cool. Once the mixture is cooled, add the clementine juice, then pour into a 700 ml (24 fl oz) sterilized bottle (see page 256). Label and store in the refrigerator for up to 2 weeks.

ORANGE AND HONEY SHRUB

- 500 g (1 lb 2 oz) oranges, chopped with peel left on
- 300 g (11 oz/1 ½ cups) caster (superfine) sugar
- 100 g (3½ oz) honey
- 500 ml (17 fl oz) cider vinegar

Muddle the oranges, sugar, honey and vinegar together in a large container, then transfer to a Thermomix® (see page 230 for alternative options) and bring to the boil. Simmer for 15 minutes on heat 2. Leave to cool. Double strain (see page 17) into a 700 ml (24 fl oz) sterilized bottle (see page 256). Label and store in the refrigerator for up to 2 weeks.

PINEAPPLE AND ROSEMARY SHRUB

- 500 g (1 lb 2 oz) pineapple, chopped with rind
- 300 g (11 oz/1 ½ cups) caster (superfine) sugar
- 100 g (3½ oz/scant ½ cup) honey
- 6 rosemary sprigs
- 500 ml (17 fl oz) cider vinegar

Muddle the pineapple, sugar, honey, rosemary and vinegar together in a large container. Place in the Thermomix® (see page 230 for alternative options) and bring to the boil. Simmer for 15 minutes on heat 2. Leave to cool. Fine strain through a muslin cloth (cheesecloth) and squeeze out all the liquid. Pour into a 700 ml (24 fl oz) sterilized bottle (see page 256). Label and store in the refrigerator for up to 2 weeks.

POMEGRANATE AND FENNEL SHRUB

- 1 litre (34 fl oz) fresh pomegranate juice
- 500 g (1 lb 2 oz) fennel bulb, chopped
- 250 g (9 oz/1 ¼ cups) caster (superfine) sugar
- 250 ml (8 fl oz) cider vinegar

Place the pomegranate juice, fennel, sugar and vinegar into a Thermomix® (see page 230 for alternative options). Set the speed to 1 and cook at 60°C (140°F) for 45 minutes. Strain into a 700 ml (24 fl oz) sterilized bottle (see page 256). Label and store in the refrigerator for up to 2 weeks.

WATERMELON AND TOMATO STALK SHRUB

- 300 ml (10 fl oz) fresh watermelon juice
- 225 ml (8 fl oz) fresh lime juice
- 10 g (¼ oz) tomato stalks (stems)
- 100 g (3½ oz/ ½ cup) caster (superfine) sugar

Place the watermelon and lime juices, tomato stalks (stems) and sugar in a large jug (pitcher) and leave to infuse for 1 hour, stirring occasionally to dissolve the sugar. Strain through a paper coffee filter into a 700 ml (24 fl oz) sterilized bottle (see page 256). Label and store in the refrigerator for up to 3 days.

SORBET

UMESHU SORBET

- 150 g (5 oz/ ¾ cup) caster (superfine) sugar
- 700 g (1 lb 8 1/2 oz) ice cubes
- 150 ml (5 fl oz) umeshu (Japanese plum wine)
- 150 ml (5 fl oz) elderflower liqueur

Place the sugar in a blender and blitz at maximum speed for 10 seconds. Add the ice, umeshu and liqueur and blend at maximum speed for 1 minute. Strain into an airtight freezerproof container and freeze for 12 hours, or until solid. Store in the freezer for up to 1 month.

SPICED

SPICED COFFEE

- 250 ml (8 fl oz) brewed espresso
- 250 ml (8 fl oz) still mineral water
- 6 black cardamom pods
- ½ tonka bean (see page 256)

Place all the ingredients in a blender and mix for 30 seconds, then leave to infuse for 10 minutes. Fine strain through a muslin cloth (cheesecloth) into a 700 ml (24 fl oz) sterilized bottle (see page 256). Label and store in the refrigerator for up to 1 week.

SPICED RICE MILK

- 750 ml (25 fl oz) still mineral water
- 360 g (12 oz/generous 1¾ cups) white rice
- 4 whole cloves
- 2 cinnamon sticks
- 500 ml (17 fl oz) rice milk
- 300 ml (10 fl oz) condensed milk

Combine the mineral water, rice, cloves, cinnamon sticks, rice milk and condensed milk in a large jug (pitcher) and mix well. Strain through a paper coffee filter into a 700 ml (24 fl oz) sterilized bottle (see page 256). Label and store in the refrigerator for up to 3 days.

VIETNAMESE PEPPER EVAPORATED AMBRATO

- 750 ml (25 fl oz) Martini Riserva Speciale Ambrato
- 3 g (¾ teaspoon) Vietnamese pepper berries

Place the Ambrato and Vietnamese pepper berries in a Thermomix® (see page 230 for alternative options) at level 2 speed at 80°C (176°F) for 1 hour. Remove from the heat and leave the mixture to cool. Fine strain through a muslin cloth (cheesecloth) into a 700 ml (24 fl oz) sterilized bottle (see page 256). Label and store in the refrigerator for up to 1 month.

SUGARS

LEMON VERBENA SUGAR

- 1 kg (2¼ lb/5 cups) caster (superfine) sugar
- 25 g (1 oz) dried lemon verbena

Mix the sugar and lemon verbena

together in an airtight container. Label and store in a cool, dry place for up to 3 months.

OLEO SACCHARUM CITRUS SUGAR

- 500 g (1 lb 2 oz/2 ½ cups) caster (superfine) sugar
- Peel of 1 orange (make sure there's no pith)
- 20 ml (¾ fl oz) macadamia oil

Combine the sugar and orange peel in a sous-vide vacuum bag (or plastic resealable bag) and seal. Leave to infuse for 24 hours, then remove the peel and add the macadamia oil. Transfer the mixture to a 700 ml (24 fl oz) sterilized bottle (see page 256) or container. Label and store in the refrigerator for up to 2 weeks.

RASPBERRY SUGAR

- 450 g (1 lb) dried raspberries
- 500 g (1 lb 2 oz/2 ½ cups) caster (superfine) sugar

Place the raspberries and sugar in a large container and, using a hand-held blender, mix together. Label and store in a 500 g (17 oz) airtight container in the refrigerator for up to 1 month.

SYRUPS

AMALFI LEMON LEAF SYRUP

- 1 litre (34 fl oz) Sugar Syrup (page 245)
- 2 drops Amalfi lemon leaf food-grade essential oil

Mix the sugar syrup and lemon oil, then pour into a 700 ml (24 fl oz) sterilized bottle (see page 256). Label and store in the refrigerator for up to 2 weeks.

BAKED LEMON SYRUP

- 1 litre (34 fl oz) Sugar Syrup (page 245)
- 50 g (2 oz) Burnt Lemon Peel (page 235)
- 3 g (⅒ oz) bamboo charcoal
- 5 drops black food colouring

Place all the ingredients together in a blender and mix, then leave to rest for 30 minutes. Fine strain through a muslin cloth (cheesecloth) into a 700 ml (17 fl oz) sterilized bottle (see page 256). Label and store at room temperature for up to 2 weeks.

BASIL AND SZECHUAN PEPPER SYRUP

- 1 litre (34 fl oz) Sugar Syrup (page 245)
- 20 g (¾ oz) Szechuan peppercorns
- 20 basil leaves

Bring the sugar syrup, Szechuan pepper and basil leaves to the boil in a saucepan. As soon as it's boiling, remove from the heat and leave to cool. Strain through a paper coffee filter into a 700 ml (24 fl oz) sterilized bottle (see page 256). Label and store in the refrigerator for up to 1 week.

BLACK CARDAMOM SEED SYRUP

- 750 ml (25 fl oz) Sugar Syrup (page 245)
- 12 black cardamom pods

Using a blender, mix the sugar syrup and cardamom pods together, then leave to infuse for 2 hours. Fine strain through a muslin cloth (cheesecloth) into a 700 ml (24 fl oz) sterilized bottle (see page 256). Label and store in the refrigerator for up to 2 weeks.

CATUABA BARK SYRUP

- 50 g (1¾ oz) catuaba bark
- 700 ml (24 fl oz) Sugar Syrup (page 245)

Place the catuaba bark and sugar syrup in a sous-vide vacuum bag (or plastic resealable bag) and seal. Cook in a sous-vide bath (see page 230 for alternative options) at 60°C (140°F) for 1 hour. Fine strain into a 700 ml (24 fl oz) sterilized bottle (see page 256). Label and store in the refrigerator for up to 2 weeks.

CHILLI SYRUP

- 700 ml (24 fl oz) Sugar Syrup (page 245)
- 2 Scotch Bonnet chillies

Add the sugar syrup and chillies to a blender and blitz until the chillies are very finely chopped. Leave to infuse for 30 minutes, then strain through a paper coffee filter into a 700 ml (24 fl oz) sterilized bottle (see page 256). Label and store in the refrigerator for up to 1 week.

EUCALYPTUS SYRUP

- 1 litre (34 fl oz) Sugar Syrup (page 245)
- 20 dried eucalyptus leaves

Place the sugar syrup and eucalyptus leaves in a large

container and leave to infuse for 24 hours. Strain through a paper coffee filter into a 700 ml (24 fl oz) sterilized bottle (see page 256). Label and store in the refrigerator for up to 2 weeks.

GINGER SYRUP

- 200 ml (7 fl oz) freshly pressed ginger juice (use a juice extractor)
- 200 ml (7 fl oz) still mineral water
- 400 g (14 oz/2 cups) caster (superfine) sugar

Add all the ingredients to a large jug (pitcher) and stir until the sugar dissolves. Strain through a paper coffee filter into a 700 ml (24 fl oz) sterilized bottle (see page 256). Label and store in the refrigerator for up to 3 days.

HOJA SANTA AND SAFFRON SYRUP

- 750 ml (25 fl oz) Sugar Syrup (page 245)
- 2 g (⅒ oz) dried hoja santa leaves
- Small pinch of saffron threads

Place the sugar syrup and hoja santa leaves in the Thermomix® (see page 230 for alternative options) and blitz at full speed. Cook the mixture at 60°C (140°F) for 30 minutes. Pour the mixture into a large container and add the saffron. Leave to cool, then strain through a paper coffee filter into a 700 ml (24 fl oz) sterilized bottle (see page 256). Label and store in the refrigerator for up to 2 weeks.

MATCHA SYRUP

- 700 ml (24 fl oz) still mineral water
- 500 g (1 lb 2 oz/2½ cups) caster (superfine) sugar
- 15 g (½ oz) matcha green tea powder

Bring the mineral water to the boil in a large saucepan, then add the sugar and tea. Return to the boil and simmer for 5 minutes. Remove from the heat and leave to cool. Fine strain through a muslin cloth (cheesecloth) into a 700 ml (24 fl oz) sterilized bottle (see page 256). Label and store in the refrigerator for up to 2 weeks.

NEPITELLA MINT SYRUP

- 12 drops nepitella or calamint food-grade essential oil
- 1 litre (34 fl oz) Sugar Syrup (page 245)

Pour the nepitella oil and sugar syrup into a 700 ml (24 fl oz) sterilized bottle (see page 256), seal and shake to combine. Label and store in the refrigerator for up to 2 weeks.

OPOPANAX SYRUP

- 12 drops opopanax food-grade essential oil
- 1 litre (34 fl oz) Sugar Syrup (page 245)

Pour the opopanax oil and sugar syrup into a 700 ml (24 fl oz) sterilized bottle (see page 256). Seal and shake to combine. Label and store in the refrigerator for up to 2 weeks.

OSMANTHUS AND TIMUR PEPPER SYRUP

- 3.5 g (1/10 oz) osmanthus flowers
- 1 g (2 barspoons) timur peppercorns
- 600 ml (20 fl oz) boiling water
- 300 g (11 oz/1 1/2 cups) caster (superfine) sugar

Place the flowers and peppercorns into a large jug (pitcher) with the boiling water and leave to infuse for 12 hours. Fine strain through a muslin cloth (cheesecloth) into a large container, add the sugar and stir until dissolved. Pour into a 700 ml (24 fl oz) sterilized bottle (see page 256). Label and store in the refrigerator for up to 2 weeks.

POMEGRANATE SYRUP

- 100 ml (3 1/2 fl oz) freshly squeezed pomegranate juice
- 300 ml (10 fl oz) Sugar Syrup (page 245)

Pour the pomegranate juice and sugar syrup into a 700 ml (24 fl oz) sterilized bottle (see page 256). Shake to combine. Label and store in the refrigerator for a maximum of 3 days.

ROSEHIP SYRUP

- 100 g (3 1/2 oz) dried rosehips
- 700 ml (24 fl oz) still mineral water
- 500 g (1 lb 2 oz/2 1/2 cups) caster (superfine) sugar
- 5 ml (1 barspoon) rose flower water

Slightly crush the rosehips and roast them for 1 minute in a large, deep saucepan over a medium heat. Pour the mineral water over the rosehips and bring to the boil, then simmer for 5 minutes. Add the sugar, bring to the boil again and simmer for another 5 minutes. Remove from the heat and leave to cool. Add the rose flower water. Strain through a muslin cloth (cheesecloth) into a 700 ml (24 fl oz) sterilized bottle (see page 256). Label and store in the refrigerator for up to 1 week.

SALTED DATE SYRUP

- 36 ml (1 1/4 fl oz) still mineral water
- 9 g (1/4 oz) salt
- 750 ml (25 fl oz) date syrup

To make a saline solution, add the water and salt to a bowl and stir until the salt has dissolved. Pour the saline solution into a 700 ml (24 fl oz) sterilized bottle (see page 256), add the date syrup and shake to blend. Label and store in the refrigerator for up to 1 week.

SUGAR SYRUP

- 500 ml (17 fl oz) still mineral water
- 1 kg (2 1/4 lb/5 cups) caster (superfine) sugar

Add the mineral water and sugar to a blender and blend until combined and the sugar has dissolved. Pour into a 700 ml (24 fl oz) sterilized bottle (see page 256). Label and store in the refrigerator for up to 1 month.

TINCTURES

COFFEE TINCTURE

- 700 ml (24 fl oz) extra dry vermouth
- 30 g (1 oz) coffee beans

Place the vermouth and coffee beans in a large container and leave to infuse for 24 hours. Strain through a paper coffee filter into a 700 ml (24 fl oz) sterilized bottle (see page 256). Label and store at room temperature for up to 1 month.

SAGE TINCTURE

- 500 ml (17 fl oz) blanco tequila
- 100 g (3 1/2 oz) fresh sage leaves

Place the tequila and sage leaves in a sous-vide vacuum bag (or plastic resealable bag) and seal. Cook in a sous-vide bath (see page 230 for alternative options) at 60°C (140°F) for 1 hour. Strain through a paper coffee filter into a 700 ml

(24 fl oz) sterilized bottle (see page 256). Label and store at room temperature for up to 1 month.

WINES

BLUE SANCERRE WINE

- 10 ml (2 barspoons) blue food colouring
- 700 ml (24 fl oz) Sancerre wine

Combine the blue food colouring and wine in a large jug (pitcher). Pour into a 700 ml (24 fl oz) sterilized bottle (see page 256). Label and store in the refrigerator for up to 1 week.

EVANISH BORDEAUX WINE

- 750 ml (25 fl oz) Bordeaux wine

Pour the wine into a large saucepan and bring to the boil, then reduce the heat and simmer until the volume is reduced by half. Pour into a 700 ml (24 fl oz) sterilized bottle (see page 256). Label and store in the refrigerator for up to 1 week.

SPARKLING STRAWBERRY WINE

- 500 ml (17 fl oz) Chablis wine
- 150 ml (5 fl oz) strawberry purée
- 100 ml (3 1/2 fl oz) Sugar Syrup (page 245)

Place the wine, purée and sugar syrup into a soda container. Stir and mix well. Charge in a carbonation machine (we use a large pipe attached to a CO_2 canister) or use a soda siphon. Refrigerate. You can store the soda water without charging it in a 700 ml (24 fl oz) sterilized bottle (see page 256) in the refrigerator for up to 1 week.

ABOUT THE AUTHORS

AGOSTINO PERRONE

With an eye for the aesthetic and a passion for creativity, Ago first mixed drinks in a local café in his birthplace, Lake Como, Italy, to fund his photography studies. The art of bartending immediately got into his blood. In 2003, he moved to London, honing his skills alongside the capital's best bartenders. In 2006, he led the opening of Montgomery Place, in Notting Hill, London, and was named CLASS Bartender of the Year in 2006. Beginning to collaborate with Italian spirits companies, he combined two dreams – to travel the world and to discover new ingredients and cultures. Approached by the Connaught hotel in 2008, he formed the opening team of the eponymous bar's launch to bring his bright and innovative approach to five-star hotel mixology. Ago and the Connaught Bar team have built an unparalleled hospitality legacy, awarded numerous accolades, including top ten ranking in the World's 50 Best Bars from 2009 to 2022 – number 1 in 2020 and 2021. Ago's work has gained international acclaim, appearing in top media and receiving the most prestigious awards, culminating in the recognition of the Industry Icon Award at the World's 50 Best Bars 2022 and Best International Bar Mentor at Tales of the Cocktail 2023.

GIORGIO BARGIANI

Coming from a family background in hospitality, Giorgio grew up in Pisa, Italy, where he gained his understanding and passion for restaurants and bars. He had also enrolled to study business and communication, before hearing the call to enter into hospitality. Cutting his teeth in the luxury hotel industry, working at The Splendido Hotel in Portofino and Le Manoir aux Quat'Saisons in Oxfordshire, he arrived at the Connaught Bar as a barback in 2014. Giorgio's attention to detail, coupled with his contagious energy and creativity, led to his promotion to Head Mixologist in 2019 and Assistant Director of Mixology in 2022, as well as the accolade of International Bartender of the Year at Tales of the Cocktail 2023.

MAURA MILIA

Growing up in a small Sardinian village, Maura graduated with a degree in human sciences but quickly found herself attracted to hospitality. Having started her career journey in luxury establishments across Italy and the UK, Maura began work as a waitress at the Connaught Bar in 2014. It was love at first sight when she walked into the bar. With her distinctive drive and an innate sense of hospitality, Maura has worked her way up the ladder to become the Connaught Bar's Bar Manager. She was the recipient of the CLASS Bar Manager of the Year award in 2021.

AUTHORS' ACKNOWLEDGMENTS

A heartfelt thank you to all the people who helped create this book: Anistatia Miller for writing; Jared Brown for history inspiration; Lateef Okunnu for the photography; Astrid Stavro for the design; Emily Takoudes, Ellie Smith, Clare Churly and the Phaidon team for guidance; Laura Grassulini for supporting the vision; and Sandeep Bhalla, the Connaught hotel management, Paula Fitzherbert, the Maybourne communications and marketing team for support throughout the creation.

A great many people helped forge the Connaught Bar into the place we know today.

A special acknowledgment goes to our Connaught Bar colleagues – more than a team, a family who have made an enormous contribution to our hospitality and cocktail culture.

To the guests, friends and our partners – Gaby, Alex and Annalisa – who have shared our journey, evolution and some important, celebratory moments: we would not be here without you.

A mention to all the colleagues we have met around the world, for inspiring us and encouraging us to pursue our hospitality mission.

Finally, thanks to the Connaught Hotel and Maybourne Group family, for the support, trust and love. We hope to continue to make you as proud as you make us every day.

Straight up with style, and don't forget the smile!

Phaidon Press Limited
2 Cooperage Yard
London E15 2QR

Phaidon Press Inc.
111 Broadway
New York, NY 10006

phaidon.com

First published 2024
© 2024 Phaidon Press Limited

ISBN 978 1 83866 810 5

A CIP catalogue record for this book is
available from the British Library and the
Library of Congress.

Commissioning Editor: Emily Takoudes
Project Editor: Clare Churly
Production Controller: Lily Rodgers
Design: Astrid Stavro
Photography: Lateef Okunnu

Printed in China

PUBLISHER'S ACKNOWLEDGMENTS
Phaidon would like to thank Evelyn Battaglia,
Hilary Bird, Julia Hasting, Anistatia Miller, João
Mota, Ellie Smith, Tracey Smith and Kathy Steer.

RECIPE NOTES
- Eggs are UK size medium (US size large),
  unless otherwise specified.
- Essential oils in recipes should be food-grade
  essential oils.
- Fruit juice is always freshly squeezed, unless
  otherwise specified.
- Herbs are fresh, unless otherwise specified.
- Milk is full-fat (whole) or semi-skimmed
  (reduced-fat) milk, unless otherwise specified.
- Salt is fine sea salt, unless otherwise specified.

- Sugar is caster (superfine) sugar, unless
  otherwise specified.
- Individual vegetables and fruits, such as
  carrots and apples, are assumed to be
  medium, unless otherwise specified, and
  should be peeled and/or washed unless
  otherwise specified.
- All herbs, shoots, flowers and leaves should
  be picked fresh from a clean source and
  should be washed before using.
- Metric, imperial and cup measurements
  are used in this book. Follow one set of
  measurements throughout, not a mixture,
  as they are not interchangeable.
- All tablespoon and teaspoon measurements
  given are level, not heaped, unless otherwise
  specified. 1 teaspoon = 5 ml; 1 tablespoon =
  15 ml. Australian standard tablespoons
  are 20 ml, so Australian readers are advised
  to use 3 teaspoons in place of 1 tablespoon
  when measuring small quantities.
- When no quantity is specified, for example
  of edible powders, sprays and paints for
  finishing dishes, quantities are discretionary
  and flexible.
- Cooking and preparation times are for
  guidance only. If using a convection (fan)
  oven, follow the manufacturer's instructions
  concerning oven temperatures.
- When sterilizing bottles, wash the bottles in
  clean, hot water and rinse thoroughly. Preheat
  the oven to 140°Cc/275°F/Gas Mark 1. Place the
  bottles on a baking sheet and place in the
  oven to dry.
- Exercise a high level of caution when
  following recipes involving any potentially
  hazardous activity including the use of high
  temperatures.
- Tonka beans are prohibited from use in
  the USA. Substitute vanilla bitters for tonka
  bitters. Substitute vanilla seeds for tonka
  beans (the seeds of 2½ vanilla beans are
  equivalent to 1 grated tonka bean). When
  grated tonka beans are used as a garnish
  for cocktails, dilute the vanilla seeds in
  a neutral spirit and spray over the drink.
- Alcohol by volume (ABV) icons are for
  guidance only. The ABV of the cocktails may
  vary, depending on the ABV of the spirits used.
- Always drink responsibly.